THIRD EDITION

Management and Supervision for Working Professionals

VOLUME I

Herman Koren, R.E.H.S., M.P.H., H.S.D.
Professor of Environmental Health and Safety
  and Director Management I and II Program
Indiana State University

Recipient of National University Continuing Education Association (NUCEA)
Meritorious Course Award

May be used as a self-directed study course for earning continued education credit hours
(CEUs) through Indiana State University

NATIONAL
ENVIRONMENTAL
HEALTH ASSOCIATION

LEWIS PUBLISHERS
Boca Raton   New York   London   Tokyo

Library of Congress Cataloging-in-Publication Data

Catalog record is available from the Library of Congress

This book contains information obtained from authentic and highly regarded sources. Reprinted material is quoted with permission, and sources are indicated. A wide variety of references are listed. Reasonable efforts have been made to publish reliable data and information, but the author and the publisher cannot assume responsibility for the validity of all materials or for the consequences of their use.

Neither this book nor any part may be reproduced or transmitted in any form or by any means, electronic or mechanical, including photocopying, microfilming, and recording, or by any information storage or retrieval system, without prior permission in writing from the publisher.

CRC Press, Inc.'s consent does not extend to copying for general distribution, for promotion, for creating new works, or for resale. Specific permission must be obtained in writing from CRC Press for such copying.

Direct all inquiries to CRC Press, Inc., 2000 Corporate Blvd., N.W., Boca Raton, Florida 33431.

© 1996 by CRC Press, Inc.
Lewis Publishers is an imprint of CRC Press
© 1987 by Herman Koren
© 1980 by Indiana State University

No claim to original U.S. Government works
International Standard Book Number 1-56670-203-8
Printed in the United States of America 1 2 3 4 5 6 7 8 9 0
Printed on acid-free paper

Dear Professional:

This material may be studied in a self-directed manner or you may request examinations through Indiana State University (see forms in the back of the course material). A fee will be charged for exams leading to Continuing Education Units (CEUs) and a certificate of achievement and for recording the CEU credit.

I would like to suggest that you set a time schedule for working on each chapter, which constitutes a lesson. Two weeks for a chapter seems to be an appropriate amount of time to spend for the average student. The actual study time per chapter, however, could vary from 6 to 10 hours during this period. You will note that some chapters will require more or less time depending on the content.

Our case problems are of a general nature. For a more practical case problem, think of a case history similar to the ones used which specifically applies to your organization. Try to resolve these problems in ways that have been presented in the following course material.

Sincerely,

Herman Koren, R.E.H.S., M.P.H., H.S.D.
Professor of Environmental Health and Safety and
Director of Management I and II Program

About the Author

Herman Koren (H.S.D., Indiana University; M.P.H., University of Michigan; R.E.H.S, State of Indiana; and R.P.S., State of Pennsylvania) is a professor of Environmental Health and Safety and the Director of the Management I and II programs at Indiana State University, Terre Haute, Indiana. Dr. Koren, who has been active in the professional fields for 40 years, is a widely known author, lecturer, consultant, educator, and practitioner in the environmental health, occupational health, hospital, medical care, and safety fields. He has been a district environmentalist in both county and city health departments, a district supervisor in the Philadelphia Department of Public Health, Chief of Environmental Health and Safety at Philadelphia General Hospital, Associate in the Department of Preventive Medicine at the University of Pennsylvania Medical School, as well as being chairperson for numerous national committees and tasks forces in a variety of environmental, health, hospital, and safety areas.

He is a founder diplomate of the American Inter-Society Academy for the Certification of Sanitarians, a fellow of the American Public Health Association, and was a member of the editorial board of both the Journal of Environmental Health and the Journal of Food Protection. In addition to his years of work experience, he has also gained practical experience during his last 26 years by supervising 1150 environmental interns in 70 different health departments in a fifteen-state area. He has served as a consultant to the U.S. Enviromental Protection Agency (EPA) the National Institute of Environmental Health Science, the National Environmental Health Association, and to numerous health departments and hospitals. He is also the author of six books and numerous articles.

He is the founder of the Student National Environmental Health Association and a member of many other health organizations. He developed the concept of the environmental health practioner in hospitals, as well as the environmental health internship program for college students, acting as its coordinator at Indiana State University since 1967. At that time, he also developed the undergraduate environmental health program. In addition, Dr. Koren has enrolled over 4,000 people in the course covered in the material in *Management and Supervision for Working Professionals*, Course I. This interest was first stimulated by the need to upgrade the existing professional and nonprofessional. By doing this, he strives to understand the variety of problems which are of concern in society today. These courses are presented through Indiana State University and are open to individuals throughout the world for continuing education credit.

COURSE DESCRIPTION

Management and Supervision for Working Professionals, Volume I and Volume II, offers the reader a practical set of methods, tools, and techniques which will enable the practicing supervisor or manager, or the individual seeking to become a supervisor or manager, to better do his/her job. The courses outline ways to achieve leadership qualities, promote better human relations, improve employee morale, develop better communication skills, and learn practical and tested approaches to becoming a better supervisor. The course material is applicable to supervision and management in the fields of environmental health, environmental management, water quality, waste water, hazardous waste, public health, health care, institutional health, occupational health, safety management, nursing and nursing homes, hospitals, governmental practice, industrial management, and small businesses.

COURSE OBJECTIVES

The course objectives are to:

1. Introduce you to a set of practical, tested approaches to the vital areas of supervision and management, in an age when the worker has many rights and safeguards which have been provided by various labor laws, civil rights acts, and health and safety laws.

2. Learn the techniques of developing good human relations with your subordinates, your peers, and your supervisors.

3. Learn how to create and maintain a pleasant environment within the organization in order to achieve the organization's goals.

4. Learn about the different types of attitudes which exist, how to shape these attitudes, and how to motivate employees to perform at higher levels of accuracy and quality.

5. Understand the techniques used, for planning, organizing, and coordinating activities in your department and how to apply these techniques in a practical manner.

6. Understand when to counsel employees, how to carry out counseling, and how to recognize when the employee should be referred for additional help.

7. Learn how to develop self-discipline in the use of time and work schedules, and how to develop time and work schedules for yourself and others.

8. Learn and apply the various techniques used in oral and written communications in dealing with employees, peers, supervisors, and the general public.

9. Learn and utilize the established techniques of teaching, training new employees, and retraining or instructing existing employees.

10. Learn when and how to discipline; understand what is appropriate

discipline, and estimate what the results of the discipline will be.

11. Learn how to handle complaints and how to avoid grievances.

12. Understand the vast array of human problems and how each employee should be treated as an individual.

13. Recognize the various systems of performance ratings and learn how to give daily, weekly, monthly, and yearly performance ratings.

14. Understand your relationship with the trade union and how best to work with it in personnel matters.

15. Learn your various roles in health and safety and practical means of achieving a healthy and safe environment.

16. Understand that you, the first line supervisor, are the key to operation of the entire organization.

17. Understand that by applying the skills which you can learn in this course you should improve your ability to motivate, integrate, and modify the environment and the personnel in it in such a way that you will achieve success in your chosen field.

BECOMING A SUPERVISOR OR MANAGER

Let's meet Jane, a typical supervisor or manager. Jane was an excellent technical worker and has been promoted to supervisor or manager. She now has the responsibility of managing other people.Chances are that Jane had almost no management training and her promotion had little or nothing to do with her ability to supervise others. Jane's superiors probably did not know whether she could handle the responsibility of the position. They were primarily impressed with her technical skill and were delighted with her eagerness to work and to become an effective and productive part of the organization. For the first several months things probably went along fairly well in her new position, but then problems began to occur. She was now the loner in the group, and her work was not going the way it should. She had little idea of what was really happening, and she may have become somewhat confused and discouraged with being a supervisor.

Perhaps you have a background as an excellent technical worker just like Jane. You probably also had or will have trouble learning to be an effective supervisor or manager. Through these two courses in Management and Supervision for Working Professionals you will begin to learn how to be a more effective manager or supervisor. Managers and supervisors, as well as technicians, must be trained to do their jobs properly. Given some effective direction, as provided in this course, and given a commitment on your part to try some proven management/supervision skills, you can become considerably more effective as a supervisor or manager. Doubtless, as a result, both you and those you supervise or manage will feel better about their work.

YOU - THE ADULT STUDENT

In this learning process you will be addressed as an adult, and you must understand that this education is somewhat different from the education of children and youth. The information contained in these pages is presented for adult learners and should be both used and considered by you when teaching and working with other adults.

It is important to realize that most adults eventually reach their goals by learning from experience. The ability to relate to others and to use the art of compromise is also an important part in attaining one's goals. Each person is unique in his/her potentials and limitations. In the area of adult education, however, the following is applicable to all adults:

1. To some extent, adult behavior can be modified.

2. Adult education should help an individual, not only to develop certain skills but also to mature.

3. The adult must be given the opportunity to act in a responsible manner in all areas of his/her life, including work.

4. The adult must assume the obligation of learning in order to become a more productive person.

5. Adults have vast untapped resources of creative potential.

6. The resources should be used to benefit the individual and his/her community.

7. Every adult can learn.

8. Every adult can be taught how to use his/her natural abilities in a better way.

9. Adults learn better when they use what they learn in practical application.

10. The adult should know how to communicate in a constructive and creative manner.

11. Most people are insecure, and learning situations may create additional insecurities in the adult. By recognizing this, the supervisor should be able to use practical approaches to help the subordinate overcome these insecurities.

12. The adult who is in a learning experience must be an active participant. He/she must be able to diagnose, plan, carry out the plans, and evaluate the results.

13. Most adults have vast amounts of personnel experience. They should rely on the experience whenever and wherever possible to learn new material. It is better to take a given idea and interpret it in your own way than to simply try to memorize it.

14. Learning is a process which is accomplished by continuous repetition.

15. Although adults tend to learn more slowly than young people, they retain newly learned material for much longer periods of time.

16. Behavior is conditioned by your feelings, emotions, environment, and past experiences as well as by reasoning and rational judgement.

17. All people seek fulfillment and happiness. This fulfillment and happiness can be achieved, in part, by understanding and by carrying out your job in the best possible way.

18. This course on supervision and management is designed to help you achieve happiness in your work, in your relationships with others, and in you home by providing a basic set of practical guidelines to help you improve in a variety of important areas.

STRUCTURE OF THE STUDYGUIDE

Management and Supervision for Working Professionals, Volume I and II, have been divided into units consisting of nine lessons and two examinations per course. The two examinations are only for those individuals who wish to enroll at Indiana State University for C.E.U.s (continuing education units).

Each of the nine lessons is presented within nine main parts:

1. The outline of the lesson tells you what you are going to be learning and in what sequence. It gives you an overall view of important items in that particular topic. The outline ends with a summary of the material which has been discussed.

2. The learning objectives provide a look at the concepts you should be learning during each lesson. You should read the objectives before you start your lesson - then go back after the lesson is

completed and read the objectives again. Make sure the material provided is clearly understood.

3. The section on Fundamental Management Information is a brief composite of material gleaned from the literature, digested by the author, and presented in such a manner that the modern manager can more effectively use his/her time without resorting to outside reading assignments.

4. The lesson discussion is taken from the author's 40 years of supervisory and management experience, a very effective course in supervision which was developed and taught by the author to individuals in various health care areas, with practical experience and ideas from a variety of different sources.

It is presumed that many who take this course will have been introduced to their supervisory experience much like the author was. At the age of 26, the author became a supervisor of a health district where he was responsible for seventeen professional employees and environmental health programs for a population of a quarter of a million people. He was made a supervisor because he was a good technician, but he was never given supervisory or administrative training. In the years since then, the author has learned, frequently the hard way, that supervision and management are specific jobs which require a special set of tools in order to be performed properly. In addition, the author has had the opportunity to develop many new techniques of supervision and evaluation of competencies of individuals in a variety of jobs.

These experiences and techniques have been incorporated into the lesson discussion which is highly readable and practical. For example, the lesson discussion states that for the supervisor to improve his/her communications skills he/she should consider the following:

- Plan what you are going to say and how you are going to say it.

- Explain your thoughts as clearly as possible in short clear words.

- Direct your message at the individual.

- Use visual aids where needed.

- Listen carefully to the worker's response to you.

- Double check to make sure the worker understands.

- Back your communications with specific actions.

- Evaluate the final actions.

By evaluating your techniques of communication versus the items stated, you can determine you own weaknesses in communications. Each time a problem is presented, practical techniques are given on how to improve the situation.

The lesson discussion serves as a practical "down-to-earth" guide on how to deal with the problems of management and supervision, offering a variety of techniques for improving your management and supervisory skills to enable you to resolve these problems. The last part of the lesson discussion summarizes the key points of the lesson.

5. The case problems and case problem questions are used by the student to get insight into the material which has been studied. All case problems of necessity are general in nature.

6. A sheet is provided at the appropriate point for answering the questions to the case problems. After completing the case problem worksheets, the student should then evaluate his/her answers against those given and, if necessary, go back to the case problem and reread it.

7. The practical exercises section gives you a series of projects to try in your own work. These projects, which are very small in scope, are based on the materials which has been presented in the lesson. For example, one lesson states that there are eight rules to be used when communicating with the public. The practical exercise or project would be to make a list of these eight items on a sheet and evaluate your performance as well as your employees' performance against these items.

The list is as follows:

• Only give out favorable information.

• Present only the facts.

• Avoid bad publicity by not giving out partial information.

• Never tell a reporter anything off the record.

• Inform the public and press of public-spirited enterprise.

• Make sure your company speakers understand company policy.

• If you do not know the answer to a question, do not bluff, find it out.

• Always be prompt, pleasant, and accurate in dealing with the public.

Many other projects or practical exercises are mentioned throughout the lessons. You are to do two practical exercises for each lesson.

8. A sheet is provided for answering the practical exercises.

9. Self-testing examinations appear at the end of each lesson. These exercises are true-false questions. They include questions from the lessons. After you have completed the answer form by entering the responses you think are correct, you should compare your response with the correct answers. The answer sheet will, in addition, indicate the part of the lesson where the correct answer may be found. This is another means of reinforcing the material to be learned. **Do not submit these self testing questions.** These are for your own evaluation of your comprehension of the lesson content. The Midterm and Final Exams will contain true and false as well as multiple-choice questions with content somewhat more comprehensive than the self-testing examinations.

HOW TO USE THE STUDYGUIDE

The best way to use the study guide is to follow the process which has just been outlined under the STRUCTURE OF THE STUDYGUIDE. Follow it in chronological order starting with the outline first and working through to the self-testing examinations. Where you feel you have a weakness, it is wise to return to that particular section and reread it.

The studyguide can also be used as a reference book for helping to find solutions to on-the-job problems in various aspects of the supervisory role.

SUPERVISED EXAMS

Two supervised exams are required to complete each volume of the course. The Midterm is scheduled after Lesson 5 and the Final Exam after Lesson 9, which will be comprehensive for the course. Approximately 25% of the final exam questions will come from lessons 1 - 5. Forms for requesting these exams are included at the back of the course material. Each exam will be evaluated by the University. For all examinations the student will be given a letter which will provide both the grade for the examination and information on "areas of weakness" as evidenced by the exam. When you receive your letter, you should then go back and reread the material under areas of weakness. After all, even though you want to achieve a good grade on your exams, your ultimate objective should be to learn the material and be able to apply it in a practical and effective manner.

CERTIFICATE

A Certificate will be awarded.

CONTINUING EDUCATION UNITS (CEUs)

These two volumes may be used for self-study or as a resource for solving real work problems. They may also be used to earn CEU credit or continuing education hour credit for a variety of certifications. Five continuing education units are granted for the successful completion of this course. This corresponds to 50 continuing education hours.

GRADING SYSTEMS

The grading system is as follows:

Midterm (60 questions)*	120 points
Final (60 questions)*	120 points
	240 points

* No points awarded for 60% or below on Midterm and Final Exams. A make-up exam is required if exam score is 60% or below. Students must pass both the Midterm and Final Exams to receive a passing grade for the course.

Table of Contents
Volume I

Table of Contents
Volume II

LESSON 1

THE ORGANIZATION AND ITS STRUCTURE

LEARNING OBJECTIVES

When you have successfully completed this lesson, you should:

1. Understand the relationship between the first line supervisor and the field personnel, management personnel, and the overall organization.

2. Recognize many of the important responsibilities of the first line supervisor.

3. Understand the reason for the establishment of organizations, the types of organizations which exist, their functions, and understand that the organization is created by people in order to accomplish a goal.

4. Recognize the supervisor's place in management and the type of management role which he or she carries out.

5. Understand what the autocratic style of leadership is and why it is not satisfactory for the type of organization for which you work.

6. Understand the democratic style of leadership and the participating style of leadership and how each one works in order that you may choose your own particular style.

7. Recognize the necessity for a unity of command and control of personnel.

8. Understand why supervisors fail and thereby how to make yourself a successful supervisor.

FUNDAMENTAL MANAGEMENT INFORMATION

INTRODUCTION

The executive management team is responsible for futuristic thinking, planning, budgeting, evaluating, and redirecting the organization to meet expressed needs, objectives and stated goals. The executive management team works through a series of different management and supervisory levels.

EXECUTIVE MANAGEMENT TEAM

The executive management team is a team of people who coordinate the activities of an organization in order to meet its goals and objectives. Management is also the process of working with people to plan, organize, direct, control, and coordinate human and material resources.

An executive manager is a member of this team of decision makers. There is a hierarchy in a management team, where certain individuals have more authority than others and, therefore are responsible for running the organization and delegating authority as needed.

HIERARCHY

The term hierarchy refers to individuals at different levels of authority. Authority can be formal, which is based on the actual power in the organization, or informal,

which is obtained from other individuals when they are willing to do things for you because of your skills, their admiration for you, or because you have some other level of power in another organization.

The typical management hierarchy consists of a board of directors, the chief executive officer or administrator, the middle management team, and the first line supervisors. The top management level is responsible for proposing policy to the board based on careful analysis of a variety of situations. This chief executive officer (CEO) also recommends the appropriate budget, the goals and objectives of the planned programs, and the means for implementing the programs. It is then the function of the board to approve or reject the policies and programs. The CEO then puts the plan into action in an effective manner by use of the various management levels of the organization. It is then the function of this individual to review the evaluations of the appropriate actions related to the programs and the results of the programs to see if the objectives of the organization are being carried out. It is essential for this individual to perform in this role of futuristic thinker, planner, director, organizer, and coordinator of the work of the other individuals.

DELEGATION OF AUTHORITY

The executive manager delegates

3

authority to middle management and first line supervisors. However, the delegation of authority does not relieve the executive manager of the ultimate responsibility for what occurs. This is called accountability. Each individual that exercises any type of authority must then be held accountable for the results as well as the cost of the program.

MIDDLE MANAGEMENT

The middle management group is made up of individuals responsible for specific program areas. These individuals must be capable of taking the plan and program of the top management and interpreting it to the supervisors within the department and to the professionals and other members of the staff working at a field level. The middle manager must also be able to plan the activities based on the program plan, and control, organize and direct the work of subordinates. This individual must be able to evaluate the program and make necessary changes where needed. If the changes involve questions in the program, the middle manager should discuss this with the administrator or CEO.

LINE AND STAFF

Line managers, who tend to be generalists, are individuals who carry forth the authority from the highest level of the organization and direct the operation of the field personnel. Staff managers are specialists who assist the line managers in

carrying out their functions. The staff managers are specialists in areas such as personnel, budgeting, purchasing, human resources, and office automation.

GOALS

The purposes or goals of the organization are most important, since the results of the use of time and money will be measured against the original purposes and goals. The purposes and goals are broken down further into objectives and should be measurable

OBJECTIVES

An organization typically has short-term objectives (these are to be achieved in one year or less), intermediate objectives (these are to be achieved in one to five years), long-term objectives (these are to be achieved in five or more years). The middle managers evaluate the appropriate data to determine what would be an effective objective. They then decide what it is they wish to accomplish and how much it will cost in dollars, people, and other resources. They finally determine the specific objectives for the program. To set good objectives, the middle managers should determine how best to implement the program plan. These individuals, with the help of the executive manager, should then state very clear and specific objectives that relate to the various phases of the program. The objectives should be high enough to indicate achievement, but not so high that they will not be reached under normal circumstances. A specific time period should be established for the objectives.

The middle managers always try to be as effective as possible in reaching the objectives while also being efficient in the use of resources. Management is much more than telling people what to do. It is a complex process involving the utilization of a variety of resources in an effective manner.

MANAGEMENT BY OBJECTIVES

The approach called management by objectives, or MBO, has three main points: (1) All individuals in the organization set a specific group of objectives, which they try to reach during a specific time period; (2) There are periodic performance reviews during the course of this time period; and (3) The organization members are rewarded if they reach their specific goals.

In order for an MBO program to work, the top managers of the organization must first set appropriate goals and objectives. The managers and subordinates should work together to develop and agree upon the individual goals and objectives. The managers and subordinates must agree that the individual objectives are just and can be reached in a fair manner.

Employee performance must be evaluated carefully against the established objectives. If the employee meets the objectives, he or she should be rewarded.

The use of MBO programs have advantages and disadvantages. The organization must determine if this is the approach it wants to use.

SUMMARY

The key to management is the appropriate use of technical skills, human skills, and conceptual skills to meet the objectives of the various program areas.

LESSON DISCUSSION

I. ORGANIZATION AND THE FIRST LINE SUPERVISOR

The first line supervisor is the key person in the organization. The supervisor must be able to take the intelligent, top management decisions and put them to work with the individuals who are carrying out the task. The supervisor not only transmits information, techniques, and goals from the top to lower levels, but also must transmit needs, frustrations, requirements and thoughts of the lower-level personnel upwards towards management. The supervisor is an individual who must have adequate authority to carry out the responsibilities of his/her job. The responsibilities include such things as checking work, investigating accidents, scheduling employees, keeping records, being accountable for material and personnel, checking time cards, good housekeeping, selecting and training employees, making work assignments, maintaining discipline, handling employee problems, motivating employees, making certain production decisions, working with other departments and coordinating the efforts of all the departments, and producing either services or products with maximum efficiency and at a minimum cost. The first line supervisor is the key to the operation.

II. THE ORGANIZATION

Our society is a social organization. We band together to achieve common goals because of a common interest for self-preservation, for protection, and for a means of exchanging goods and services to achieve a better way of life. We pay, play, and pray in organizations. The organization is created by us and in the end may make us a slave to the creation. Even when we die, the state - which is an organization - must grant permission for burial or disposal.

**Banding Together
To Achieve A Common Goal**

Organizations vary from the different levels of government to our social societies and country clubs. The reasons organizations exist are as varied as the types of organizations. For the purpose of this course on Management and Supervision, we will discuss the organization as it relates to management, supervisors, and the individuals being supervised. Managers are also supervisors. We are of necessity concerned with business, industry institutions, labor unions, governmental bodies, and so on.

Our society places a high moral value on being rational, effective, and efficient. At present, the organization is the most rational and efficient form of social grouping. As a result of this and in order to meet the needs of our modern society, organizations have increased sharply in numbers and in complexity.

The functions of the organization are to:

1. Coordinate a large number of human actions.

2. Create a powerful social tool which can be used to achieve some result for the group of individuals in the organization.

3. Combine personnel and resources by weaving together the leaders, experts, workers, machines, and raw materials, in order to produce various products as well as services for the society.

4. Constantly evaluate itself and attempt to adjust itself to achieve its goals.

5. Be a more efficient operation than smaller natural groupings such as families, friendship groups, and communities.

The organization attempts to define relationships between people in the organization, the organization itself, and other groups. The individuals set up objectives, rules and regulations, and perhaps finally a charter or constitution. In setting up the organization people give up some power and freedom of choice in order to give the organization the ability to operate. For instance, when the Constitution of the United States was drafted, individuals as well as independent states relinquished powers to the federal government. This allowed that organization, the federal government, to function effectively in protecting the health and welfare of the individual states and people.

As a result of the bringing together of all of the individuals and resources, the organization becomes more effective than each individual or large groups of individuals. The organization is able to utilize the tools of planning, coordinating, controlling, and evaluating to develop an effective program.

Unfortunately, as individuals give up freedom and power, they may become frustrated with their inability to make the organization work in the manner which they intended. The more complex the organization, the greater the loss of freedom and the greater the chance workers will become frustrated. Eventually, the organization can become the master instead of the servant, and the individuals must then become subservient to the organization. In the very beginning of our country, our society was rural and, therefore, not very complex. Along with the industrial revolution our society has become far more complex; the federal and state governments, which are our major organizations, have now become masters instead of servants.

Organizations such as the federal and state governments are broken down into smaller groupings such as the Department of Labor, Department of Commerce, Environmental Protection Agency, and so on. Unfortunately, the rules and regulations issued by the various departments many times conflict with each other or bring about a social and human condition which is unacceptable to us.

Span of Control: In order to strengthen the organization, the span of control of any given manager or supervisor must be decided. It is suggested that six to ten individuals should be under the immediate supervision of a supervisor and no more than six to ten supervisors should report to a manager. By exercising this type of span of control the organization is able to operate more effectively.

Line and Staff Personnel: Since it is impossible, unrealistic, or simply not a good idea to have everyone act as a specialist, the organization is broken down into two separate groupings. The line personnel are those who are supposed to accomplish the goals of the organization. The staff personnel are generally specialists who are supposed to help the line personnel carry out their jobs effectively. Unfortunately, in many areas there is a conflict between the line and staff personnel. This conflict leads to confusion and also contributes to poor performance.

Remember: Organizations are artificial creatures which people put together in order to accomplish specific objectives such as providing safety, health, goods, or services. In order for the organization to function the people in it must be organized and supervised. The supervisor must also be supervised. The organization is an effective means of achieving goals, but it reduces the freedom of the individuals involved.

III. THE SUPERVISOR'S PLACE IN MANAGEMENT

The supervisor as a leader has the same functions of planning, organizing, directing, and controlling as other members of the management team. However, management is usually divided into supervision, middle management, and top management. The first level manager or supervisor is important since he or she is the one who is most directly involved with the workers. Therefore, the first level supervisor has to carry out orders of the higher levels of management in such a way as to get the workers to perform their jobs in an efficient and orderly manner. The techniques utilized will be discussed in several other sections of this course. Supervisors tend to be generalists whereas the higher level management may be specialists. The supervisor must have an understanding of each of the jobs of the individuals working for him or her and must be able to teach these individuals how to perform their jobs in a satisfactory manner.

**Supervisors Must
Transmit Information
From Top To Lower Level**

IV. LEADERSHIP STYLES

A. The autocratic leader assumes full authority and full responsibility for whatever occurs and offers penalties and rewards based upon employee performance. The penalties may be reprimands, layoffs, or firings. The rewards may be bonuses or an increase in salary. Unfortunately, in many cases autocratic leadership "rules by fear". This develops frustration which may lead to aggression and conflict. It stifles the creativity of the individual, and it causes the individual to work only because he or she has to, not because he/she wants to. This form of leadership, although practiced by certain supervisors, is certainly not recommended.

B. The democratic leader believes that the best way to produce is to create a climate where employees want to do their best to meet the objectives and goals of the organization. Decisions are arrived at after consulting with the subordinates, and there is general agreement on how to achieve the necessary goals that have been set forth. The individual is respected and may be able to produce a good product with a happy group of workers. Unfortunately, this too may have its drawbacks since there is no clear-cut leader who takes control of the situation and makes the necessary decisions. If the workers are not really interested in participating and if the leadership is weak, this form of leadership may also fail.

C. Participation is the best form of leadership. In a typical democratic approach individuals share in the responsibility of the work and help make decisions concerning how to obtain the goals outlined by the company. The leader is strong and is able to guide the individuals into utilizing their skills to be productive and happy in their jobs. Successful participation is based on the following principles:

1. There must be time to participate before the action is carried out.

9

2. The financial cost of individual participation should not exceed its economic or other values.

3. The work the individuals are participating in must be relevant to what they do.

4. The participant must have the ability, intelligence, and the knowledge necessary to participate and express ideas clearly.

5. None of the parties should be threatened by this exchange.

Participation in management can eliminate much of the complaining, griping, and accidents attributed to dull, repetitive, seemingly meaningless jobs that offer little or no challenge.

V. UNITY OF COMMAND AND CONTROL

An employee should receive orders from one superior only. When two or more bosses are involved, the subordinate may become confused and frustrated in trying to decide which order to follow. Many times the employee is left to make his/her own decisions when the supervisors disagree and give counter orders or assignments. The employee may then be criticized for not obeying the orders, when in fact he/she is obeying one order but cannot obey conflicting orders. When two supervisors share in the supervision of one employee, it becomes very difficult to give a proper performance rating or to assist the employee in improving his/her job performance.

VI. WHY SUPERVISORS AND MANAGERS FAIL

Supervisors fail because of:

1. Poor personal relationships with the workers or with other management personnel.

2. Lack of initiative, emotional instability, and other personal traits.

3. Lack of understanding of the management's or the board's point of view.

4. An unwillingness to spend the necessary time and effort to improve themselves.

5. A lack of skill in planning and organizing work.

6. An inability to adjust to new and changing conditions.

7. They are the wrong persons for the job.

Just because you are an excellent technical person does not mean you will automatically be a good supervisor or manager.

VII. SUMMARY

The "Fundamental Management Information" section sets forth a basic understanding of management, what it does, and how it works.

This Lesson Discussion has laid the groundwork for the rest of the course by introducing the concepts of different types of organizations, what they are made of, how they function, how they set goals and attempt to achieve them.

The supervisor's place in management and in the organization has been looked at from two points of view, from the organization's and from the supervisor's. Different types of leadership styles have been referred to and their strengths and weaknesses have been explored. Several key points concerning why supervisors and managers fail have been listed.

In following lessons various aspects of supervision and management will be discussed in considerable depth.

LESSON 1
CASE PROBLEM 1

The New E.R. Director

Dr. John Tarry was the new Emergency Room director at the Wilson County Hospital. Dr. Tarry felt that his education and experience in the military was superior to those of the emergency room staff. He immediately advised the staff that there would be a meeting at 0800 hours the following day. At the meeting he stated that all decisions concerning budget, hiring of employees, patient care, and employee discipline would be made by him personally. Further, anyone forgetting to enter any items on the computer, making any errors in patient care, or neglecting to complete charts would be subject to immediate disciplinary action. In the following two weeks he ordered one-day suspensions for three nurses and an E.M.T. He criticized both the patient care manager, and the supervising nurse in front of the staff. The supervising nurse, patient care manager and five nurses went to the hospital administrator, Mr. Harwell, and turned in their resignations.

1. What did Dr.Tarry do wrong when he became the emergency room director?

2. What leadership style was he demonstrating?

3. How would he have handled this situation if he were a participation leader?

4. If you were the administrator, what would you do?

ANSWER SHEET

LESSON 1
CASE PROBLEM 1

MANAGEMENT AND SUPERVISION FOR WORKING PROFESSIONALS

LESSON 1
CASE PROBLEM 2

Why Supervisors Fail

Joe Brown was the first line supervisor at the Plain City waste water treatment plant. Joe managed 10 employees and in turn was responsible to both Rita Forrest and Tim Smith. Joe was always irritable with his employees and demanded that they perform at a high level of efficiency while he himself showed a lack of personal initiative. He was confused by the conflicting orders given to him by Rita and Tim. He never truly understood the company policy and did not care to spend the time to clarify the situation. He was totally disorganized. His annual performance rating was unsatisfactory.

1. What kind of management traits was Joe lacking?

2. Was he set up for failure? Why?

3. Was Joe the right person for the job?

4. How could the city have helped Joe be more successful?

ANSWER SHEET

**LESSON 1
CASE PROBLEM 2**

MANAGEMENT AND SUPERVISION FOR WORKING PROFESSIONALS

PRACTICAL EXERCISES

You may do any two or more of these items.

1. Make a check list of the responsibilities the normal first line supervisor has in an organization and determine how many of these responsibilities apply to you. This should give you some indication as to the type of supervisory job you would hold.

2. Use the list of types of organizations from the lesson discussion and add others as necessary. Evaluate these organizations to determine how they achieve their goals. Find the first line supervisor type in each of these organizations and compare them to you and your responsibilities.

3. Evaluate your role in your organization versus the role of other supervisors in a variety of other organizations. This should help to show you that you are not too different from other individuals. Although we like to be unique, it is also important to know that we face the same problems as others.

4. Evaluate your organization to determine who fits the role of autocratic leader, who fits the role of the participating leader. Evaluate their work as well as you can, the responses from others, and whether they are successful or not as a supervisor or manager. In turn evaluate your own role to see which category you would fall into.

5. Make a list of the successful principles of participation. Determine if this list is applicable to your leadership style and organization.

6. Determine the type of command and control utilized in your organization and whether or not it is too broad or too narrow. If it appears to be too broad, determine if this is causing problems in decision making or if it is causing problems with the employees.

7. Make a list of the items under "Why Supervisors Fail." Each day for a period of two weeks check whether or not you have fallen into any of these categories. If you have, evaluate why this is occurring and take necessary steps to improve your supervisory skills.

LESSON 1
PRACTICAL EXERCISES ANSWER SHEET

MANAGEMENT AND SUPERVISION FOR WORKING PROFESSIONALS

Do two exercises and number them. Use additional paper if necessary.

SELF-TESTING EXAMINATION #1

TRUE-FALSE QUESTIONS (CORRECT ANSWERS APPEAR ON PAGE 20)

1. A manager is a member of the team of decision makers.   1. __

2. Delegation of authority relieves the management of responsibility for decisions.   2. __

3. Staff members are specialists who aid in carrying out functions.   3. __

4. Informal authority is not important in an organization.   4. __

5. Intermediate objectives typically are for a 1-2 year period.   5. __

6. The MBO program is based solely on the employee's perception.   6. __

7. The first line supervisor, who is the key person in the organization, is
    involved in selection and training of employees.   7. __

8. The first line supervisor is never involved in making production decisions.   8. __

9. The function of an organization is to coordinate a large number of unit actions.   9. __

10. The organization is a formal structure which is set up by people to accomplish
    certain specific goals.   10. __

11. Organizations are artificial creatures which people put together.   11. __

12. Organizations include such groups as the chamber of commerce, charities,
    community groups, industries, and so on.   12. __

13. The supervisor has the same basic functions as the manager in directing and
    controlling, but not in planning or organizing.   13. __

14. The first line supervisor has to understand the jobs of each of the individuals
    working for him or her.   14. __

15. The autocratic leader is superior to the democratic leader since he/she is able
    to obtain immediate results.   15. __

16. Participation is the least desirable form of leadership.   16. __

ANSWERS TO LESSON 1 SELF-TESTING EXAMINATION

If your answer is incorrect, go back to the material referred to and determine why your answer is incorrect.

QUESTIONS FROM FUNDAMENTAL MANAGEMENT INFORMATION SECTION

1. __T__ Beginning of Fundamental Management Information
2. __F__ Beginning of Fundamental Management Information
3. __T__ Middle of Fundamental Management Information
4. __F__ Middle of Fundamental Management Information
5. __F__ Middle of Fundamental Management Information
6. __F__ End of Fundamental Management Information

QUESTIONS FROM LESSON DISCUSSION SECTION

7. __T__ Beginning of the Lesson Discussion
8. __F__ Beginning of the Lesson Discussion
9. __T__ Beginning of the Lesson Discussion
10. __T__ Beginning of the Lesson Discussion
11. __T__ Beginning of the Lesson Discussion
12. __T__ Beginning of the Lesson Discussion
13. __F__ Middle of the Lesson Discussion
14. __T__ Middle of the Lesson Discussion
15. __F__ Middle of the Lesson Discussion
16. __F__ Middle of the Lesson Discussion

CASE PROBLEM 1 ANSWERS

The New E.R. Director

1. He tried to run the E.R. like it was a military operation. He expected everyone to be perfect and to accept any order or decision he made. He gave no thought to anyone's feelings when he criticized them in front of others. He felt he was superior to everyone else in the E.R.

2. Autocratic style of management

3. He should have met with the entire staff and observed the operation for at least six to eight weeks. He then should have met with the patient care manager and supervising nurse to discuss any possible changes in current procedures. All employees then should have been notified, retrained, and given time to adjust to the changes. These changes should have been approved by the nursing supervisor.

4. The employees should be asked to delay their resignations until the problems can be investigated and resolved. The administrator should then counsel Dr. Terry. He should be advised that the administrative function of the E.R. belongs to the nursing supervisor, but his recommendations and suggestions to her would be appreciated, when related to medical decisions. The staff should be reassured and appreciation should be shown for their effort. If Dr. Terry still can not change his approach he should be transferred to another position, with different responsibilities.

CASE PROBLEM 2 ANSWERS

Why Supervisors Fail

1. Joe had a lack of personal initiative. He was irritable with employees, apathetic, disorganized, and a poor role model.

2. He was set up for failure because his attitude and performance were poor. He answered to two supervisors who gave him conflicting orders. He never really understood the company policy and did not care whether or not he did.

3. He was the wrong person for the job.

4. He should have been trained to understand all the jobs, company policies, goals, and objectives. His role needed to be clarified and the line of supervision simplified. He should have been given supervisory and management training.

LESSON 2

WHAT IS SUPERVISION AND MANAGEMENT?

LEARNING OBJECTIVES

When you have successfully completed this lesson, you should:

1. Understand the difference between managers and supervisors, and recognize what your role should be.

2. Learn why supervisors are the key individuals in an operation.

3. Recognize that the supervisor must learn the art of supervision.

4. Learn how to use the techniques of planning, organizing, directing, and controlling to become a more effective supervisor.

5. Recognize the supervisor's role as a problem solver.

6. Understand the four essential needs of the new supervisor.

7. Learn how to set goals and how to use the goal-setting process.

8. Learn how to use the decision-making process.

9. Recognize that you became a supervisor or manager, and others became supervisors or managers, basically because you were and are a skilled worker and not because you were a professional in the art of supervision.

FUNDAMENTAL MANAGEMENT INFORMATION

INTRODUCTION

Leadership is the process of directing the behavior of others toward the accomplishment of an objective. It is the ability to get work done with and through others, while winning their respect, confidence, loyalty, support, and cooperation. The leader seeks to get voluntary participation by subordinates. Leading is not the same as managing. Leading emphasizes behavioral issues where as managing emphasizes the assessment of the situation, the selection of goals, the development of means of achieving these goals, the use of resources, the design, organization, direction, and control of people in order to cause the programs to be successful. A good leader tends to be intelligent, emotionally mature and stable, dependable, hard working, and persistent. He or she has the ability to work with the individuals, to make them comfortable in what they are doing, and to urge them on to success.

ART OF LEADERSHIP

Leadership is an art that can be acquired. The effective leader has excellent technical skills, is supported by considerable general knowledge, and has a good command of the English language. He or she has a desire to accomplish, a willingness to be flexible, the ability to urge, direct, and assist people, the ability to remove himself or herself from the situation to look at things in proper perspective, and the ability to do the right things at the right times. A good leader needs good followers who are knowledgeable, work together, accept challenges, and who learn and give appropriate feedback to the leader. All leaders are limited by their knowledge, skills, attitudes, and abilities as well as by their own weaknesses and inadequacies. They are limited by the groups over which they have authority. Their level of experience, proficiency, and skill have to be greater than the subordinates in order to lead well. Leaders are also limited by the resources available, including people, and the special conditions that may be part of the problem or program. The key to effective leadership is the ability to learn from current situations, to adapt this knowledge to future problems, and to convince people to act in a positive manner.

LEADERSHIP STYLES

There are four different types of leadership styles:

1. Directive leadership: where the individual tells the subordinates what is expected of them and provides specific guidance, schedules, rules, regulations, and standards;

2. Supportive leadership: where the individual treats the subordinates as equals;

3. Participative leadership: where the leader consults with the subordinates to find solutions to problems and to help make decisions;

4. Achievement oriented leadership: where the individual sets challenging goals, emphasizes the necessity to continually improve, and tries to maintain a high degree of confidence in the subordinates.

IMPLEMENTATION OF DECISIONS

The leader, who of course is the manager, arrives at decisions in a variety of ways and then attempts to implement them. Implementation techniques utilized are as follows:

1. The individual makes the decision and announces it to the group.

2. The individual sells the decision to the group.

3. The individual presents his or her ideas and asks for group reaction to the possible decision.

4. The individual presents a tentative decision to the group which is subject to change based on group analysis and discussion.

5. The individual presents the problem, gets a series of suggestions from group members and then arrives at a decision.

6. The individual defines the limits of the problem an asks the group to make the decision.

7. The individual allows the group to make decisions within certain limits.

SUMMARY

The effective manager is a successful leader who has the ability to get others to carry out a variety of tasks in a positive manner because they want to do it. He or she has the qualities needed to encourage subordinates to work toward meeting the goals and objectives of the organization.

LESSON DISCUSSION

I. THE DIFFERENCE BETWEEN MANAGERS AND SUPERVISORS

A. Managers create and maintain an atmosphere where people can perform in an efficient way in order to achieve the goals of the company. This atmosphere is part of the internal environment which is better known as the organization. Management coordinates the human and material resources in such a way as to help the individuals work toward the company goal. In effect, management is the process in which unrelated resources are integrated into a meaningful operation. Obviously, these definitions are brief and general in nature. However, remember that managers are also supervisors.

B. Supervisors have some of the basic roles as managers in controlling, planning, organizing, and directing - but they do it at a different level. Supervisors have a major function in leading, stimulating, motivating, coordinating, and directing the work of other individuals in such a way that these individuals can produce adequate goods and services and work toward the goals of the organization. Furthermore, whereas management is more concerned with markets, money, and public relations, supervision is most concerned with the people who actually carry out the necessary tasks. A supervisor works within a given situation and, therefore, must be able to perform in an effective manner as the situation changes in nature. The successful supervisor has special characteristics such as adaptability, empathy, and the ability to understand changes in the work situation. An understanding of changes in the work situation should be reflected in the supervisor's method of making assignments to employees. The supervisor is the first one to analyze a problem and determine what type of solution is necessary.

II. THE NEED FOR SUPERVISION

The supervisory job came from the idea that someone had to give direction in order for a group to work in an effective manner. When you place twenty people outside in a snow-shoveling job, twenty will work as individuals. If one of the twenty becomes a supervisor, then the supervisor can direct and coordinate the efforts of the other nineteen to get the job to flow in a smooth manner in order to effectively remove the snow. This is a common example of why a supervisor is needed and why the position was originally created. You only need to watch a group of children playing and you will see that one assumes the role of being in charge. This is a typical happening. In order for a group to stay together, the supervisor has to be a binding force. The supervisor has to be able to set a common objective for everyone and then encourage the individuals to commit themselves to work toward this objective. The supervisor also becomes the individual who takes the efforts of a variety of individuals (each having a variety of different

27

talents) and organizes them into a purposeful, meaningful approach. The supervisor satisfies the need of the group because he/she can give direction and can also confer recognition upon the group. As any good athletic coach knows, teamwork is required to win. The objective of supervision is to get the team to pull together.

A. The key person in an entire operation is the supervisor. Although he or she is primarily concerned with helping subordinates carry out their functions, the supervisor is also consulted on general problems within the organization. The supervisor is the line of communication between the subordinates and the managers - the individual who establishes the tone of the organization at the most important level, where the work actually gets done. If the supervisor sets a good example and shows continuing enthusiasm, then the workers will certainly assist the supervisor in reaching the goals of the organization. For the worker, the immediate supervisor has to be the most important individual in the organization since the worker takes his/her orders from the immediate supervisor. For the supervisor, the most important person is the middle manager, and so forth. It is to this supervisor that the worker goes to for instruction, information, and guidance in personal affairs from time to time. The worker complains to his/her supervisor, asks for raises and favors, converses with the supervisor, and produces with the supervisor. This individual, the supervisor, has to keep management and the subordinates reasonably satisfied and still

carry out personal responsibilities.

III. SUPERVISION AND MANAGEMENT AS A PROFESSION

Although supervision is as much a profession as any of the other trade or science areas, the supervisor typically does not receive adequate training and therefore must develop supervisory skills through trial and error. Some industries provide supervisory training for young men and women who appear to have excellent potential. In most cases the individual is able to survive the problems created in the supervisory role through trial and error and, hopefully, by being blessed with a good personality and a keen sense of understanding of individuals. People involved in supervision should be given necessary training. It is the intent of this course to help provide the necessary training for existing and future supervisors and managers.

IV. THE ART OF SUPERVISION AND MANAGEMENT

Supervision is an art. The worker who anticipates moving upward in the organization should carefully observe good and bad supervisors and managers. This will offer an opportunity to learn some of the techniques of supervision. The observation of a good supervisor or manager is important since the individual may want to copy techniques. The observation of a bad supervisor or a manager is important since

28

the individual is given an opportunity to see what occurs when bad supervision is practiced. Thus, one can then take the opportunity to do just the opposite of the bad supervisor or manager. Older supervisor or managers may be very useful since they have seen many different situations. If possible, you should discuss your problems and your techniques with an older supervisor or manager and seek his/her help in planning your approach toward the resolution of the problems. The key to the art of supervision and management is to be a decent person who is straightforward and helpful--but firm.

V. PUTTING IT ALL TOGETHER

The good supervisor is able to clearly understand his or her own duties and responsibilities and the duties and responsibilities of subordinates. The supervisor must realize where and what his/her prerogatives, rights, and authority are. The supervisor needs to communicate with subordinates. The supervisor must be able to evaluate, motivate, and when necessary, discipline. The major kinds of work carried out by the supervisor include:

A. *Planning* - The supervisor plans his/her work and the work for subordinates.

B. *Organizing* - The supervisor organizes the work of subordinates, decides which individuals will carry out specific tasks, and obtains necessary space, materials, and equipment. He/she develops procedures and methods and works within the proper time

schedule and budget.

C. *Directing* - The supervisor, on a one-to-one basis, furnishes the necessary leadership on an hourly, daily, weekly, and monthly basis in order to motivate the subordinate to use his or her skills to carry out functions properly.

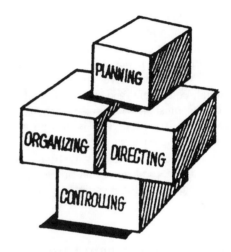

Putting It All Together

D. *Controlling* - The supervisor controls the work of the employees and makes sure that the organization's plans are carried out properly. The supervisor sets forth the standards of performance, helps the individual comply with these standards, and provides the necessary evaluation to make sure that the work is done properly.

The supervisor, in putting it all together, has to give endless attention and careful guidance to workers. Care must be taken to

29

avoid antagonizing the individual worker. The supervisor must continuously motivate workers to do an appropriate and effective job.

VI. THE SUPERVISOR AS A PROBLEM SOLVER

The supervisor is deeply involved in solving the problems related to meeting goals of planning, organizing, directing, and controlling on a day-to-day basis. The supervisor must solve problems with material, equipment, and space. Most of all, he or she must solve human problems. In many cases, the supervisor is in a position where there is no clear-cut or easy way to resolve problems. It is only through good judgment and good sense that problems are resolved, allowing the organization to move forward.

VII. THE NEW SUPERVISOR

The new supervisor must have the following essentials ready to utilize in order to do the job properly.

1. Job knowledge - This knowledge must not only include his/her former job, but it must also include a general knowledge of all the other jobs performed by new subordinates. The supervisor must have the ability to make good, sound, technical decisions and the confidence to convince subordinates that his/her decisions are good ones.

2. Assistance - The supervisor must receive assistance from others. The managers, the co-supervisors, and others must continuously give their support and advice and help the new supervisor when he/she makes mistakes and when employees react in an adverse manner toward the supervisor.

3. Education - The supervisor must have a good education because a supervisor is constantly involved in communications, paper work, formal reports, and so on. The supervisor is the spokesperson and therefore must be able to speak in a clear, concise, and grammatically correct manner.

4. Success - The supervisor must have a strong desire to succeed. This desire can mean the difference between failure and success. Everyone has shortcomings. The smart supervisor is able to overcome shortcomings by learning quickly, by using good judgment, and by having a desire to be the best in his or her work. There is no reason why the smart individual who has the skills to work with others cannot succeed in the role of supervisor.

The new supervisor must work on improving his/her personal relations with others, individual shortcomings, lack of understanding of what is needed, lack of skill in planning and organizing, and the lack of ability to adjust to new and changing conditions as rapidly as possible.

VIII. GOAL SETTING AND THE GOAL-SETTING PROCESS

Goal setting by the supervisor must fit into the overall goals or objectives of the organization. The organization and its members should work together to achieve their common goals. The best technique for setting goals is as follows:

1. Set forth the purpose of the work to be done.

2. Establish specific goals to carry out this purpose.

3. Determine the importance of these goals.

4. Make plans for action.

5. Develop performance standards and criteria for measurement.

6. Set forth anticipated problems.

7. Determine the amount of resources needed to carry out planned action.

8. Set forth ultimate plans.

9. Provide a way for the individual to interact with the organization.

10. Follow up with an actual performance evaluation.

When setting goals, specific ones should be set forth for short-range and long-range periods of time. These goals should be clearly thought out in advance. The short-range goals should be determined by various levels of management and supervision in order to meet the long-range goals of the organization. Specific performance standards and target dates which are realistic should be established to meet the given goal. If short-range goals are not being realized, then the supervisor as well as the various levels of management should review the situation and determine the problems.

IX. THE DECISION-MAKING PROCESS

Supervisors are constantly making decisions. A proper decision-making process involves the following steps:

1. Recognizing and analyzing of the problem.

2. Determining workable solutions.

3. Identifying the key areas of uncertainty.

4. Gathering the necessary data.

5. Estimating whether or not an alternative is workable.

6. Choosing a proper solution.

7. Taking the necessary action.

8. Following up the action.

X. HOW YOU BECOME A SUPERVISOR

The chances are that you were a very skilled worker in your particular area and that you had performed at a very high level. Therefore, you were recognized by your employer and promoted to supervisor of your unit. Unfortunately, chances are that you had virtually no management training and your promotion had nothing to do with your ability to supervise or manage. You may not have wanted to become a supervisor or manager, but when offered the position you saw that it was an opportunity to make additional money and to advance yourself in the organization. The skilled individual who is motivated and exhibits great zeal in his/her work is sought after by management for promotional opportunities. However, this same individual may not have the training or even the necessary skills to become a proper supervisor. Management also noticed that you got along quite well with people and despite the fact that you were one of the group you were able to maintain your high peak of performance.

Now you are no longer the laboratory worker, you are the laboratory supervisor. You are no longer the nurse, but now the nursing supervisor. You are no longer the housekeeper, but the housekeeping supervisor. You are no longer the maintenance man, but now the maintenance foreman. You are now in a position where you are the leader instead of one who is being led.

Ladder Climbing
Some Fall Off The Ladder
Some Go To The Top

When you assumed the title, your world changed. There was a short period when everyone congratulated you, told you how good you were, and noted the fact that you really understood people, their qualities, and how best to get the most work done in a pleasant manner. In the beginning you may even have remained part of the group you were working with. However, the situation changed. Suddenly you were in charge, the supervisor! Problems were occurring! People were not reacting to you properly! Employers were not satisfied with you! Life was no longer as comfortable as it had been before. The fact is that becoming a new supervisor can be extremely traumatic for it can cause a crisis in your life and even in your association with your family. Your former stability and security have been threatened.

It is necessary for you to understand that you can become a good supervisor. What you need is proper training and experience in the art of supervision.

XI. SUMMARY

The "Fundamental Management Information" section discusses types of leadership and decision making.

This lesson has described the difference between managers and supervisors. It has shown that managers are also supervisors and that everything which applies to the supervisor also applies to the manager, but at a higher level. It has established the role of the supervisor, the need for supervision, the art and techniques of supervision and management, the problems of the new supervisor, the techniques used to establish goals and make decisions, and finally it has given you some insight into how a supervisor is chosen. In the succeeding chapters the course will describe techniques of successful supervision and management. It will provide for you a basis for becoming what you want to be - the successful, confident, supervisor or manager for today and tomorrow.

LESSON 2
CASE PROBLEM 1

The Decision-Making Process

Harry and Jean, supervisors at the Pine County Health Department, were being considered for the vacant position of Director of Environmental Health. The interview board posed the following problem to determine the clarity of their thinking and their ability to make decisions under stressful conditions:

The State Health Department has ordered the county to develop and start a new program on underground storage tank surveillance within 90 days to comply with U.S.E.P.A. requirements. No additional funds will be available. The existing staff will have to modify on-going required programs in order to satisfy this new requirement. If you were Harry or Jean how would you deal with the following:

1. Determine which programs to cut back.

2. Decide which staff individuals should be assigned to the new program.

3. Choose a proper solution to the problem.

4. Develop appropriate goals and objectives for all of the problemmatic areas under the new conditions.

5. Determine what other means of funding may be available to operate in an efficient manner.

ANSWER SHEET

LESSON 2
CASE PROBLEM 1

MANAGEMENT AND SUPERVISION FOR WORKING PROFESSIONALS

LESSON 2
CASE PROBLEM 2

Putting It All Together

As a recent graduate of State University, Cora was the supervisor of Hopping Nursing Care Service. Cora spent most of her time in her office reviewing documents and reports. She also frequently attended meetings away from the organization. Her fifteen employees developed and carried out their own programs. They set up their own schedules and made whatever decisions were necessary. At the end of six months, both the quality and quantity of work had deteriorated substantially. Cora was asked by her director, Mr. Albert, to submit a report on how she was carrying out her role of supervisor in the areas of planning, organizing, directing, and controlling.

1. If you were Cora what changes would you make in:
    a. Effective planning of operations.
    b. Helping subordinates organize their work in an effective way.
    c. Directing the work of the department.
    d. Controlling the operation.

2. What did Cora do wrong in her role as a supervisor?

3. What did Mr. Albert do wrong in his role as a manager?

ANSWER SHEET

LESSON 2
CASE PROBLEM 2

MANAGEMENT AND SUPERVISION FOR WORKING PROFESSIONALS

PRACTICAL EXERCISES

You may do any two or more of these items.

1. Make a list of your basic role in management including controlling, planning, organizing, leading, stimulating, motivating, and coordinating. Determine what you do in each of these areas, how you go about doing it, and whether or not you are being successful. Make this same list for an individual that you consider to be a supervisor. Compare yours to his/hers in order that you may be able to see your strengths and weaknesses.

2. Prepare a chart for a two-week period. Briefly write down each problem brought to you by your employees or by your superiors. Write down how you handled each of the problems and whether or not you were successful.

3. Evaluate yourself to determine if you presently have the four major qualities needed to be a good supervisor. These include job knowledge, the ability to give assistance, adequate education, and a strong desire to succeed.

4. Determine for a one-week period whether or not your personal relations with others are good. Where you think you have done something which has been successful, where individuals have been motivated to work, or where the end product was useful, give yourself a plus and write down the situation. At the end of one week, you will begin to see how you are relating to other individuals and whether your relationship is more to the plus or minus side. It is then necessary to enhance the good qualities and improve upon your weaknesses.

5. Set forth your goals for your work based on principles noted in the Lesson Discussion. Take the ten major items of goal setting and apply them to a specific area with which you are concerned. Decide if you have followed each of these ten recommendations. If you have not, determine why not, and then make plans to make the necessary corrections.

6. The decision-making process is essential for a good supervisor. Analyze three major decisions which you have made within the last week and see if you have followed each of the eight steps which are stipulated in the lesson discussion. If you have not and the decision was a good decision, determine if you may have followed these steps in an informal rather than formal manner. If your decisions were not as good as they could be, go back and read the decision-making process again.

7. For the next major decision that you need to make, set up the eight steps in a decision-making process and follow them carefully.

8. Determine why you were made a supervisor and whether or not you had any formal supervisory training prior to the elevation in position.

LESSON 2
PRACTICAL EXERCISES ANSWER SHEET

MANAGEMENT AND SUPERVISION FOR WORKING PROFESSIONALS

Do two exercises and number them. Use additional paper if necessary.

SELF-TESTING EXAMINATION #2

TRUE-FALSE QUESTIONS (CORRECT ANSWERS APPEAR ON PAGE 43)

1. Leading is the same as management.   1. __

2. Directive leadership is where the individual treats the subordinates as equals. 2. __

3. The effective leader has considerable general knowledge.   3. __

4. A good leader can take poorly trained people and be successful.   4. __

5. A good leader tries to modify behavior to improve skills.   5. __

6. A form of decision making involves defining the limits of the problem and
    asking the group to make the decision.   6. __

7. The function of management is to coordinate the human and material
    resources of the company in such a way that the individuals will work
    toward the company goal.   7. __

8. Supervisors have a major function in learning, stimulating, and motivating but
    they are not involved in coordinating and directing the work of others.   8. __

9. Management is more concerned with markets, money, and public relations while
    supervisors are most concerned with the people who carry out the work.   9. __

10. The supervisor is the first one to analyze a problem and to make some
    determination on how to solve it.   10. __

11. The supervisor's job is primarily to make the work flow in a smooth and
    even manner in order to achieve the goals of the organization.   11. __

12. The supervisor has generally learned the skills of supervision
    through trial and error.   12. __

13. Supervision is an art and therefore has to be developed through learning good
    techniques and practicing them within specific situations.   13. __

14. The good supervisor is not involved in planning since this is part of the management process.   14. ___

15. The supervisor solves problems on a day-to-day basis.   15. ___

ANSWERS TO LESSON 2 SELF-TESTING EXAMINATION

If your answer is incorrect, go back to the material referred to and determine why your answer is incorrect.

QUESTIONS FROM FUNDAMENTAL MANAGEMENT INFORMATION SECTION

1. T Beginning of Fundamental Management Information
2. F Beginning of Fundamental Management Information
3. T Beginning of Fundamental Management Information
4. F Beginning of Fundamental Management Information
5. T Beginning of Fundamental Management Information
6. T Beginning of Fundamental Management Information

QUESTIONS FROM THE LESSON DISCUSSION

7.   T Beginning of Lesson Discussion
8.   F Beginning of Lesson Discussion
9.   T Beginning of Lesson Discussion
10. T Beginning of Lesson Discussion
11. T Beginning of Lesson Discussion
12. T Beginning of Lesson Discussion
13. T Beginning of Lesson Discussion
14. F Beginning of Lesson Discussion
15. T Beginning of Lesson Discussion

CASE PROBLEM 1 ANSWERS

The Decision-Making Process

1. Look at all programs. Evaluate the number of staff in each area and what they are doing. What are the legal requirements concerning what must be done and how frequently? Develop a small committee of 3-5 staff (representatives of each program) to help determine where cuts can be made. Find out how many people can be saved from each program area. Prioritize the programs and develop the proposal for maintaining existing programs while starting new ones.

2. Choose which staff individuals should be assigned to the new program. Ask for volunteers; choose staff with previous background in new programs; train individuals with good basic skills; and offer some form of recognition for working in the new area.

3. Collect all existing data about other programs similar to the one being started (networking), and add information which will customize your program. Develop appropriate and realistic budgets and reasonable objectives.

4. Meet with staff to establish goals and objectives after all data have been collected and analyzed. Make sure that the new goals and objectives are consistent with current operations and the number of people available. Make sure all objectives are measurable.

5. Review past funding of services for possibilities for new programs. Network to determine how others pay for this type of program. Find out if there are available grants or loans for the program. Determine if licensing or special taxes can help pay for the bill.

CASE PROBLEM 2 ANSWERS

Putting It All Together

1. Cora should establish programs, goals, objectives, and deadlines and issue a full report to the employees. She should work with employees to find trouble spots and determine how to set up an effective organization. She should be available to make decisions and assist in decision making. She should frequently check on the progress of the program management.

2. Cora did not perform in her role as a supervisor. She was insecure, out of touch, and lacked initiative to do the job. She did not ask for direction from her manager. She assumed that the employees could handle the work without her input, or direct involvement. She delegated responsibility, but did not evaluate to determine if the work was being done properly.

3. Mr. Albert waited too long to evaluate Cora. He should have offered her assistance and direction since she was inexperienced. He should have followed up at the first sign of deteriorating work. He should have given Cora guidance in planning, organization, direction, and controlling.

LESSON 3

WHAT IS SUCCESSFUL SUPERVISION AND MANAGEMENT?

LEARNING OBJECTIVES

When you have successfully completed this lesson, you should:

1. Understand the many qualities which are important for you to become a good supervisor.

2. Recognize the use of time as one of the most important tools in the art of supervision.

3. Understand various techniques used to train supervisors.

4. Have learned how to make proper decisions.

5. Have learned how and when to delegate authority.

6. Understand the role of public relations in the image and success of the organization.

7. Have learned how to give instructions in a clear and satisfactory manner.

8. Recognize that getting cooperation from individuals is a better means of achieving the proper goals than attempting to force the individuals into doing things against their will.

9. Have learned how to stimulate creative thinking on the part of the employees and to get them to present their useful ideas.

10. Have learned how to get along with your boss and understand what he/she expects of you and what you expect from your supervisor in return.

FUNDAMENTAL MANAGEMENT INFORMATION

INTRODUCTION

The primary function of supervisors of all types is leadership and management in a people-oriented environment. The supervisor who is going to be successful must understand people, why they work or do not work, and what is needed to motivate these individuals on a day-to-day basis. The good supervisor is an effective planner of work, a source of technical knowledge, and a mediator between management that sets the policy and the employees who make the programs work. The supervisor needs to develop a climate with good human relations at the departmental level. The supervisor will help shape the attitudes and motivate the employees toward better performance. He or she must interpret and apply company policies, specific ordinances, rules, and tasks which are needed in the given program. The supervisor trains the new employees and instructs the older employees on work effectiveness, efficiency, and safety. The supervisor counsels and disciplines employees and initiates or recommends personnel action such as promotion, transfer, and merit pay. The supervisor plans and maintains time and work schedules and adjusts them as needed based on knowledge of the specific situation. It is the function of the supervisor to make sure that the quality of service and the final product is in keeping with the high quality expected from the organization. The supervisor is the conduit through which information flows from the higher levels of administration to the individuals in the program areas and vice versa.

The supervisor has responsibility to subordinates, to peers, and also to supervisors. He or she is the individual who deals with all groups in order to keep the work flowing in a smooth and even manner. The employee reports to the supervisor and the supervisor reports to the middle manager, who then reports to the top administrative officer.

RESPONSIBILITY TO SUBORDINATES

The supervisor needs to know each of the subordinates as individual human beings. Each person has specific needs and wants and certain expectations from work. Each individual works for many more reasons than just earning a living although the money is essential to maintain life and health. If we worked only for money, many of us would leave our positions and go to jobs that paid more, but which give us less personal satisfaction. Hence, the smart supervisor will try to enhance the work experience of each of the individuals and create an environment which will be happy and challenging.

In order to develop rapport with subordinates, the supervisor must also understand the principles of good communications, which includes being a good listener. Subordinates want to know

49

that the supervisors care about them and are prepared to assist them when needed. This does not mean that the supervisor digs into the personal affairs of the subordinates but rather is sensitive to their needs and concerns.

Not all subordinates are willing to become familiar with their immediate supervisors. As a result of this, the supervisor must be careful not to step on the individual's rights and to respect the individual's privacy.

The supervisor should make sure that the individual fits the job and makes whatever adjustments necessary. If this is not possible, it may be wise to transfer the individual to a different task. The supervisor needs to back up the subordinate when the individual has carried out specific instructions in an appropriate manner and is being criticized for doing this by other individuals or the public. If it is necessary to critically review a subordinate, it should never be done in front of other people. It should always be done very gently. If the first critical review is not effective then it is necessary to start the process of reviewing the situation with some form of further action if it is needed. All of this should be documented in writing. If the supervisor offers constructive criticism, he or she should also offer adequate instructions and training on how to make necessary changes in work habits or work performance. The handling of complaints and problems in a fair and just way creates a good atmosphere for the entire group. Handled poorly it

causes dissension and ends up in grievances.

The supervisor must always be conscious of protecting and promoting the health and welfare of the subordinates while they are on work assignments. The most important thing the supervisor can do is set an example of good behavior. The supervisor should never be late or absent unless there is a specific reason for such. Never ask your employees to do things which you, yourself, will not do.

RESPONSIBILITY TO PEERS

The supervisor's peers are fellow supervisors of different departments. They can directly or indirectly affect the outcome of the program. The peers can act as a network of assistance to the supervisor or manager and help the individual in situations where the peers have personal experience. The supervisor's responsibility to peers is to know and understand each of the individuals, communicate and cooperate with them in an effective manner, and provide as much help as possible when needed. Cooperation and teamwork leads to good morale and motivation, and in the end is very helpful to the supervisor when he or she is trying to be successful.

RESPONSIBILITY TO HIGHER LEVEL MANAGEMENT

The supervisor has responsibility to managers who are both in a line and staff function. These responsibilities include:

1. Transmitting information about problems, along with recommendations for resolving them.

2. Operating within the budget which has been allotted to the program.

3. Enforcing company policy.

4. Promoting goals and objectives of the organization.

5. Attempting to be as efficient and effective as possible.

6. Maintaining all records and reports and providing these as needed in proper format and on time.

7. Utilizing the skills of people and other resources effectively.

8. Developing appropriate work schedules to meet deadlines.

9. Providing the necessary cooperation to higher level people.

THE SUPERVISOR'S ROLES

The supervisor has many roles. These include using time in an effective and efficient manner, delegating authority, good public relations, turning policy into programs, giving appropriate instructions in an effective manner, getting cooperation from people, getting useful ideas from employees, getting along with supervisors, and above all exhibiting a constant level of enthusiasm. Enthusiasm begets enthusiasm. It is contagious, in a good sense. At times the supervisor, because of having to serve so many different roles, will find that he or she is in conflict with one or more of these hats he or she is wearing in order to get the job done.

These role conflicts have to be resolved and the supervisor should turn to higher management levels to ask for help and direction when it is needed.

SUMMARY

Supervisors in industry, health care settings, or government are the most important part of the management team, since they carry out the major functions of leading, coordinating, and directing the work of others in order to achieve the groups' goals.

They are closest to the actual work being performed and therefore are in a position to understand quickly whether or not problems exist, and recommend how to handle them.

LESSON DISCUSSION

I. INTRODUCTION

MANAGEMENT AND SUPERVISION IS	
What?	Selecting, teaching, measuring, rating people, correcting, eliminating, commending, rewarding, harmonizing, respecting, planning, and organizing.
How?	Fairly, patiently, and tactfully.
Along With:	Time, material, and money.
Purpose:	Motivating people to do their assigned tasks.
Result:	Achieving the organization's goals skillfully, accurately, intelligently, enthusiastically, and completely.

II. SIX QUALITIES IMPORTANT TO SUCCESS AS A SUPERVISOR

Thoroughness - especially in obtaining all necessary details and in using adequate base information.

Fairness - equal treatment for all employees. Investigate problems carefully because poor performance may be due to poor equipment, poor lighting, inadequate materials, or improper instruction.

Initiative - assume responsibility and start and do things without prodding. The supervisor needs self confidence, which is based on knowledge, experience (know your job), and practice in decision making. Take care to manage your own life first.

Poorly managed personal finances or family problems affect work productivity.

Tact - make employees feel important about their jobs. Constructively criticize the work and not the worker and respect the employee as an individual.

Emotional Control - control and channel your emotions and do not allow your emotions to control you. Emotions cannot be eliminated, but remember that emotional control is not based on how you feel, but on how you act, what you say, and how you say it. The four rules for gaining self-control are to recognize the importance of self-control, wait a second or two before responding when you are emotionally upset, when irritated over little things try to relax physically - if this can be done, emotional stability will soon follow. Look at your troubles in retrospect. Avoid worrying by listening to all the possible consequences. Work on more reasonable consequences and disregard the worst possible ones (if they happen you need not worry anymore).

Enthusiasm - enthusiasm can help you conquer many faults. Enthusiasm is contagious and will rid you of that "old tired feeling." It will help you gain promotions and promote self-confidence and self-satisfaction.

III. TIME AS A TOOL

One of the supervisor's most important assets is the ability to make time work in his/her favor. By doing this, the supervisor is able to work at a higher level of efficiency and is able to inspire others to work at a high level of efficiency.

Time as a Tool

It is clearly evident that many individuals in our modern society constantly waste time. In fact, the newly hired person is indoctrinated into time-killing routines. Unfortunately, this has led to numerous problems - including reduction in work efficiency and an increase in inflation. It is necessary to turn this time management condition around and make time the slave or the servant and not the master. The key to accomplishing this is through self-discipline. The supervisor must utilize the following approaches:

1. Measure time utilized for each activity,
2. Set priorities,
3. Ration your time,
4. Schedule your work, and
5. Delegate responsibilities wherever and whenever possible.

A good approach to determining how much time is used on various activities is to set up a chart by day, week, and month. Analyze how much time you use in each activity in each particular 15-minute period. Determine how much of your time is used for planning, for assembling materials and goods in preparation for the work, and how much time is used in each of the actual work activities. For the supervisor it is important to determine how much time is used for opening and reading mail, dictating responses, attending meetings, holding conferences, and in the actual work of supervision. If you do this for a period of one week, you will soon find out that much of the time that is available to you during the week is being wasted. The way to avoid this waste is to set priorities. Determine what is most important to you during that particular time period, what you must accomplish what can be postponed, and what can be delegated. It would be wise at the beginning of each day to take five minutes, close your eyes, and quietly plan what you are going to do in the course of the day. Later, write down what you have accomplished, analyze this information, and determine what you did not accomplish and determine why. You may find that the jobs that are most boring to you are being put off. You may also be putting off decisions which you are afraid to make or unable to make. It is best, once you have determined where your time is spent and if it is being spent   inefficiently, to discuss the time problem with your supervisor and ask for recommendations on how best to use and manage your time.

Another technique for time management might be to allow a certain amount of time, possibly 30 minutes or so, for looking at your mail and dictating answers. Answer the mail as it comes in so that you do not have to go back and reread it a second time. Unless business magazines being sent to you contain material that is essential, you should examine the table of contents of each magazine quickly and then place it in a pile of material for later reading. If you can use a secretary to answer correspondence or to pre-sort your mail, this is a valuable assistance.

In order to get the best performance from your workers, you should ask them to determine the best and most efficient way for them to utilize their time and explain how you can, as their supervisor, give them necessary assistance to make their time more meaningful. A busy worker performing a constructive task will be a happy worker. A worker who has to watch the clock because of boredom with a task will be an unhappy and a less confident worker.

Scheduling is the most important single thing that you can do to improve your time management. However, recognize that when scheduling you must learn to expect the unexpected. When this occurs, it is wise to accept the problem, handle it with as little frustration as possible, and then get back to the routine you have established.

Try to find shortcuts to utilize each of your assigned tasks. Utilize the time saved from the shortcuts for working with your subordinates and helping them in every way possible.

IV. EDUCATION FOR THE SUPERVISOR

In addition to learning from the older established supervisors and from working with your colleagues in order to improve your art of supervision and management, it is important to develop a very definitive education program to improve yourself. In order to find what area is most important to you, you should sit down with the outline of the various topics within this course and ask yourself, "Which of these topics constitute my biggest problems?" Then, you must ask yourself, "How can I find ways to resolve these problems?" Once you have established the problems and some of the techniques there are several ways in which you may improve yourself.

You can read selective material in a rapid manner. By enrolling in a speed reading course at an accredited center or at a local college, you may be able to increase your reading speed of 200 words per minute to a level of more than 800 words per minute.

You might be able to participate in a group of industry activities; particularly those activities in which individuals are giving down-to-earth presentations on various special problems in supervision or special problems in industry. Be active in community affairs. This gives you an opportunity to step out of your role as a supervisor and see how you fit into the overall community at large. Attend classes which will be meaningful to you. These can be at a college level, community college level, technical school level, or continuing education level. Talk to and watch others in operation. This will be of considerable value to you.

V. MAKING THE RIGHT DECISIONS

The supervisor who gets things done is the one who knows how to act decisively and how to act in a proper manner. Before you act, you must think. You must determine what you are trying to do, how are you planning to achieve it, who is going to be involved, why you are going to do it,

where the decision takes you, and when is the best time to carry out the decision.

The chronological sequence of steps varies from time to time in decision making, but the following list usually applies.

- Get the right questions. You may have several problems instead of one big problem. Therefore, you may be making a series of decisions instead of one.

- List all the facts that you need in order to make a good decision. It is a good idea to put the facts down on paper so that you actually see what the facts are. If you see the facts, you may find that you need to gather further information in order to make a proper decision.

- Carefully examine all of the information, possible solutions, and the potential ramifications from the solutions.

- Outline the pros and cons of each solution based on the previous study.

- Select the best solution. Make sure you will be able to live with the solution without worrying. Make sure as you make your selection that it is a logical decision and not an emotional one. Do not make a hasty decision. Relax before you make your final deliberation. Study any solutions that do not seem to go along with your decision. Double check all of the ramifications of your decision.

- Make your decision and act upon it. If it works, you made the right decision. If it does not work, then it is time to reevaluate it, to get more information, and then to make a different decision.

Taking no action at all is the worst way to make your decision. Do not allow someone else to make your decisions for you. In the long run, he/she may be earning your salary.

VI. DELEGATING AUTHORITY

Delegating your authority to other people will give you added hours so that you can truly carry out your functions of planning, controlling, and proper supervising. When you delegate authority wisely, you will create a situation where one or more people can carry on your job in the event of illness, an accident, or when you wish to take a worry-free vacation. The first step of delegation is the hardest one of all. This is when you must make the decision to let others do some of the work. It is not easy to let go. If you are a successful leader, you must accept and support the decisions and actions of those who make them in your name. This makes the delegation even harder since you know that the ultimate responsibility will come back to you. However, you must understand that when you do delegate authority, you do not surrender your rights and

responsibilities to others. You are not only accountable for what is done, but you also have the right to change what is being done.

An important factor in delegation is to thoroughly know the capabilities of the person to whom you delegate your authority. You should understand this individual's training, interests, likes and dislikes, and capabilities. You should list this person's strengths and weaknesses and evaluate them before making your decision to delegate, You must give to this individual all of the facts about his/her responsibility and provide him or her with a clear understanding of what they are to do and how to do it. Tell them how much responsibility and authority they have. You must also make sure that all those working for you will continue to work for this individual and follow the rules that you have set forth.

It is essential to impress upon all the workers the importance of following the established routine. Each worker must understand that the acting supervisor carries the same authority as the supervisor and, that you want them to give the acting supervisor their assistance in the same way they would give it to you.

When you have given this authority to another individual, do not get involved in the operation. Give the individual an opportunity to perform and perform well. Give him/her an opportunity to do what is necessary to come up with a good product. Leave your door open so that the acting supervisor may come in and you may help him/her make decisions.

When mistakes occur, do not take over right away. You will undermine the confidence of the acting supervisor and lower his/her prestige among the other workers. Mistakes will happen, especially among people who do not have your experience or knowledge. The smart individual will learn from mistakes. You can aid by correcting him/her in a tactful manner. In a reasonable period of time the individual should be able to perform at a decent level.

Some individuals are unable to delegate authority. They believe that if they do the job themselves it will be done right, and if someone else does it, it will not be done properly. There is no question that a good, well-trained supervisor will be able to do the job better than the untrained acting supervisor. However, at some point the supervisor must have the time to make other kinds of decisions. The supervisor must be able to leave the operation and have time to sit down and reflect upon the problems which are occurring. This means that the individual who cannot delegate authority will not only work constantly, but will probably be carrying a briefcase home every single evening in order to keep up with the work of the program. A good supervisor does not have twenty phone calls going constantly and a desk full of papers. A good supervisor will delegate part of the responsibility to other workers who show they have the ability to move into higher level positions. There is a limit as to how much authority can be delegated. Obviously, when a legal question is involved an individual cannot delegate

authority which, under law, he/she is expected to carry out. However, the individual can delegate the initial surveys, inspections, preliminary work, preliminary studies, and initial setting up of reports and techniques. All this work can be handled by others and presented in an acceptable manner to the supervisor. The Management and Supervision Volume II material will show how to prepare and present reports.

The development of subordinate supervisors is carried out by setting up a training program similar to the one you are involved in now. This training gives the individual tools and techniques necessary to carry out the many-faceted roles of the supervisor.

VII. PUBLIC RELATIONS

Training should be offered on carrying out good public relations. Many times it is public relations which gets individuals to pay attention to you and initiates work on a project. Good public relations can create good employer-employee relationships when the new person begins on the job. Public relations can make individuals in your community and within your institution or company aware of you and the institution or company and can help to create positive attitudes about both. Good public relations is meaningless if what follows the public relations is poor.

An institution or company may establish good public relations through newspaper ads, magazine ads, radio commercials, brochures, handbills, and other forms of communications. An organization's best means of public relations is to have a good product or service which is always consistent and pleases the public. The supervisor does not normally use mass media to create a good public image. His/her job is to put out a good product or service which is always reliable and consistent in quality.

Although the physical conditions of the job may change, the hours may change and the salary may change. If the supervisor maintains a good image and a good level of performance, the employees will find that the supervisor is a very stable and important part of their lives.

All employees at one time or another gripe about the person in charge. When the employees gripe about the person in charge but still have respect for him/her, the supervisor has then achieved a good public relations image.

In order to keep the employees informed and to build the necessary rapport between employees, supervisors, and managers, many organizations sponsor some after-hour social contacts such as bowling leagues, or dinners. The reason for these contacts is not only to have fun but also to show the workers that the supervisory and administrative personnel are accessible, they are human, and most certainly they are a part of the overall group.

It is essential to keep employees informed of what is pertinent in institution or company policy. Employees have a grapevine which will furnish them considerable information. It is necessary that the information be offered in an accurate and simple manner so that the employees understand what is occurring and not what the rumor mill has created. Part of keeping the employees informed is to post notices, to give them notices in their paychecks, and to have the supervisor hold periodic meetings with the employees to bring them up to date. Also developing an interesting, brief, and informative institution or company newspaper that will help the employees understand the accomplishments of the organization and give them pride in what they are doing would be a good form of personal relations.

A very excellent approach is to have an employee lunch or dinner each year. At this luncheon or dinner, employees who have performed extraordinarily during the year should be given recognition by both the organization management and supervisors. They should be given special awards, monetary awards, the opportunity to enjoy not only the event but also each other and the management personal. The cost of luncheons or dinners is negligible compared to the amount of rapport which is built as a result of the celebration.

Proper employee training, which will be discussed in another lesson, is another effective means of developing good public relations between the individual and the institution or company. This training gives the individual, from the time he/she starts work, an opportunity to know what the institution or company does, what his/her job is, and how the individual fits into the total picture. Each individual must have some feeling that the work he/she is doing is important. Otherwise, the worker will develop poor attitudes and poor morale which in turn will reduce his/her effectiveness within the organization.

When the employees or supervisor come in contact with the public there are several rules which should be followed to create a good public image for the organization. They are as follows:

1. The employee should show an interest in the consumer's problem.

2. The employee should know what he/she is talking about and be able to give a good and informative answer to the consumer.

3. If the employee does not have an answer, the consumer should be informed in a nice manner and be referred to the proper department.

4. The employee's courteous and friendly manner of speech is essential.

5. The employee must always be polite.

6. The employee's appearance should be acceptable to the public and represent the institution or the company in a proper manner.

VIII. POLICY INTO ACTION

The institution or company policy is a broad set of rules and guides which is used to achieve the goals and objectives of the organization. The policy offers a guide for supervisors as well as for managers to follow. Many policies give the supervisors the chance to use his or her own best judgment. Other policies are fixed and firm and must be followed precisely. The policy is generally set by the high-level managers or administrators and covers everything from the legal holidays which the organization will follow to the method of purchasing materials, technique for hiring and firing personnel, and the legal aspects of the organization. The supervisor is most often involved in employee policies which include wages and salaries, holidays, vacations, leaves of absence, termination of employment, insurance, hospitalization, and retirement. The supervisor will also be concerned with the policies related to requisitioning of supplies, recordkeeping, maintenance and repair of equipment, and security and safety.

Not all policies are in writing. This may be either good or bad depending on the type and the policy and the situation involved. Sometimes a policy is so rigid that there is not room for innovation or necessary change. This type of policy, unless it is an absolute requirement of the organization, would be better as an oral policy.

Policies are positive as well as negative. Policies reflect the understanding, concern and feelings of the organization. Policies of the organization should provide a channel of open communication of ideas and information upwards, downwards, and sidewards. Policies in an organization should encourage individuals to improve themselves.

The supervisor does not change the existing policy, but rather interprets it. Where a policy does not exist the supervisor may even set the policy at his/her particular level. One of the frustrations of management is that policy is set and handed down and by the time it reaches the lower level supervisory groups the policy has been altered by intermediate management and supervisors to suit themselves. This is a situation where management is losing effective control of the organization. On the other hand, if the policy went down as set forth by management and there was no opportunity for some flexibility to enforce the policy, the situation would be just as bad.

All policies should be included in a work or employee manual. This manual should spell out very clearly what the institution or company expects of you and what you can expect from them. It should state in precise language such things as vacations, days off, sick leave, and other types of situations. It should also state in precise language the route to follow for grievances, complaints, and the steps in

disciplinary action. It should describe how to advance yourself and the rewards that you will receive for advancement.

IX. HOW TO GIVE INSTRUCTIONS

When you give instructions or orders, be specific about what the employee should do and what you will expect. Make sure that you select the proper person to carry out the instructions.

Be confident and calm but avoid being cocky or offensive as you give orders. Make sure that the orders can be followed and that you are not asking for the impossible. Always check to see that the order has been carried out. Repeat your instructions slowly and clearly to make sure they are understood. Ask the employee if he/she has any questions.

It is important to request or ask that someone do something rather than say they must do something. For instance, "Joan, will you please bring me the memorandums from Mr. Holmes?" is certainly better than saying "Joan, bring me Mr. Holmes' memorandums immediately." You will receive the memos just as quickly by using the first technique and at the same time you will find that you have a more satisfied employee. There are situations where you must issue orders or commands. This is done where a hazard is apparent and the individual must make an immediate correction.

Because the employee misses an order or does not carry out an order properly does not

mean that you have done a poor job. It might be that the employee is not paying attention, is not alert, or does not care to do the job. In situations such as this it is important to sit down with the employee to find out what the problems are. These problems may be work-related, home-related, financial, or simply due to the fact that the individual does not want to work. After you have talked to the employee about the problem and listened carefully, you may be able to correct the situation. Later on in this course and in Volume II there will be specific lessons in the proper handling of employee problems and the correct disciplinary action to take. If the employee willfully refuses to carry out an order, then you must determine if this circumstance is truly insubordination. If the order was an unfair one, if you chose the wrong person to carry out the order, if the employee really misunderstood you, or if there were other problems that preoccupied the employee and prevented him/her from carrying out your instructions, then this should not be considered insubordination. If it is simply a situation where the employee does what he/she wants to do when he/she wants to do it, then suggestions and discussions will be offered for these kinds of situations later
on during the course.

Certain orders should be put in writing, while others should be given orally. It is wise when giving orders to make a mental note of them and then later to record them. During the instruction-giving period your tone of voice, manner of presentation, and the way in which you handle yourself and the individuals you deal with are important concerns. Different groups are given instructions in different manners.

X. GETTING COOPERATION

Some people cooperate willingly all the time, others cooperate grudgingly, and some just will not cooperate with their supervisors. Part of cooperation is the establishment of good attitudes. Most individuals work and perform best when they can realize a sense of accomplishment. Everyone obviously wants to earn the best salary. However, salary is only one of the motivating factors. Employees work to satisfy their physical needs, social needs, and the need to feel important.

The best way to win the cooperation of the employees is to look at the good and bad qualities you have seen in yourself and make it a point to be sensitive to the individuals' good and bad qualities. Stop talking and listen. See what people really feel and not what words you put into their mouths, Sometimes it is necessary to be extremely firm in order to get a job done. However, firmness does not mean nastiness. You can gain your workers' respect and support if you are firm and consistent. You can cause problems by inconsistency and nastiness. The supervisor should use firmness and at the same time seek the cooperation of the individuals working for him/her in order to get the necessary job done in the allotted amount of time. The individuals should understand the goals of the organization and how important it is for them to participate in achieving the goals. You can urge the employees to do their job by inspiring them - not berating them. A good athletic coach does not beat his players over the head. He shows them their mistakes, helps them plan how to best correct mistakes, and urges them on and supports their efforts. A good athletic coach is a good supervisor, good manager, and a good teacher. All supervisors should strive to attain these qualities.

When you encourage resistance from employees it is important to spot the complaints, which may simply be healthy gripes or serious objections which should be evaluated, and, if necessary, the situation should be changed. Remember that the objections may not be realistic ones. In fact, there may be a good group of workers with one poor individual who is bringing undue pressure on the entire group. In all situations, you must have an objective look at what is happening and determine whether it is you, the work, the rules, the entire group, or one individual that is causing the problem. You should not automatically assume that the group is poor, and you must not automatically assume that you are a poor supervisor.

Techniques used for removing resistance include:

1. Try using an example of a successful individual.

2. Make a guarantee that the work will improve if the individuals work harder.

3. Try a demonstration showing the individuals how best to carry out the project.

4. Ask questions. Ask the persons what they feel is hardest about the job and why they can not do it properly.

5. Listen to them. If someone is angry, upset, or irritable, find out why this is occurring. Be friendly and try to persuade the individual to make the necessary change. You should say what you think about a situation, but be careful how you word it. Employees are least likely to cooperate with you when they are afraid, when abrupt changes in their environment or work schedule occur, when there is a change in materials, methods, or supervision, and when there is fear of ridicule and embarrassment, or fear of a layoff.

XI. GETTING USEFUL IDEAS FROM EMPLOYEES

Creative thinking does not belong to management or supervision alone. It may well come from the individuals who are carrying out the variety of tasks which are necessary to meet the goals of the organization. Creative thinking is not accomplished by sitting down at some meeting and someone saying "Let us now be creative." It is true that you can have a "think tank" type of meeting where individuals will say whatever comes into their minds. This, in turn, may trigger other ideas which will be useful. However, the employees who actually perform the service or work with the equipment and perform day-to-day tasks may see what is wrong, how the work can be improved, and how it can be expedited. These contributions and suggestions should be encouraged and when the individual has made a substantial contribution to the institution or company - either through improved production, safety, public relations, or any other meaningful area - he/she should be rewarded. Employees should understand that things can be changed and that their ideas may bring about worthwhile improvements.

The fundamentals of creative thinking are to:

- Narrow down the problem. Do not simply talk about something in a vague manner. Specifically pin-point what the actual problems are.

- Learn to concentrate. If you are attempting to be creative, you cannot be effective with excessive noise and distractions around you.
- Be persistent. Do you have a good idea? Do not let it die. Sometimes the good idea cannot be sold in the first day, the first week, the first month, or even the first year. If an idea is good enough to think about, it is good enough to work for -- try to implement it.

- Believe in yourself. You must have self-confidence about what you are doing. When the situation gets tough, you must believe that you are doing something which is correct. On the other hand, do not let self-confidence become cockiness.

- Let your unconscious do part of the work. When you get tired, the best thing to do is to quit. When you go away from the situation, you are not thinking directly about a given idea, thought, or task, but your mind is still digesting, sorting, and helping you work out the necessary solutions.

- Keep presenting ideas. If one does not work, another one may.

- Take some action by writing down an idea, Present a report or a memo - document it, support it turn it over to your supervisors or managers to evaluate, but do make sure that you have some way of backing up what you are saying. Learn how to get better ideas by using some on the following techniques:

1. Choose the right time of day to concentrate on ideas. Some people think more clearly in the early morning, others in the afternoon, or late at night. Find out what kind of person you are.

2. Build up your sources of ideas. This can be done by talking to other people, reading professional or trade journals, and by looking at a variety of sources of information.

3. Do not be afraid to work alone. Your idea may not be the same as the rest of the group. However, you may be able to develop something which will be valuable and worthwhile to the organization.

4. Practice several minutes each day on how to think. Sit down, concentrate on a given subject, and let your mind wander around in a particular area. See if something pops up. Maybe you will think of how best to set up a new filing system or how best to organize the incoming work.

5. Do not worry about the number of ideas which will be useless. Unless you concentrate and learn how to think, you will never come up with the good ideas.

6. Do not worry about the opinion of others. People who do not want to change may laugh at you, taunt you, irritate you, or just ignore you, but that is alright. If your idea is good, it is worth working toward.

7. Look for the situation where you can best utilize a new thought.

8. Learn to find your own mistakes, because by correcting your own mistakes you are in effect developing a new way or a new idea about doing things.

When you attempt to sell your own idea, you may get several reactions. One reaction may be, "No, it won't work." You might get a 'sour grapes' attitude because the other individual did not think of it first. Perhaps you may get "Congratulations! That is a great idea. You are going to make a fine contribution to our organization."

A supervisor can encourage or discourage the formation of a useful idea. It can be encouraged with a smile and a happy approach. It can be discouraged by saying it is ridiculous, costs too much, too radical, not practical, or by saying we are doing it fine the way it is now.

XII. GETTING ALONG WITH YOUR SUPERVISOR

Does getting along with your supervisor mean apple polishing? Of course not. Too often we think that a supervisor who is getting along well is not doing his/her job properly but instead is trying to snuggle up to his or her supervisor. This is not true. The supervisor who has skill in human relations with the employees should exercise the same skill in human relations with his/her supervisor.

If you are a "yes-person," you may be pleasing your supervisor, but you will not be able to advance because the supervisor is not looking for the "yes- person," but rather for the individual who is attempting to make the institution or company a real success.

You should only concern the middle manager or the manager with the big problems. You should handle the routine

problems yourself. This sometimes creates a difficulty. It is not always clear as to what is routine or procedural and what is big. This is a place where no one can give you a definitive answer. You can only learn from your own experience. The best thing to do when you were first hired - and thereafter at weekly, monthly, or other periodic meetings between the supervisors and the managers - is to set some rule as to the types of problems that
should be most frequently discussed with the managers, and what problems should be handled by the supervisors.

Does Getting Along With Your Supervisor Mean Apple Polishing?

If a manager is too busy to see you all of the time, then he/she either is overworked, not properly organized, or has considerable faith in what you are doing. The best situation is where the manager

will see you when you feel that the problem is serious enough to be brought to his/her attention. If you find that despite everything you do, the manager will not only not see you, but also will ridicule you, laugh behind your back, or attempt to tear you down as a supervisor, then it is time for you to consider changing to a new position or to recognize the situation as it stands, accept it, and go on with your own work.

Your middle manager or administrator should not only give you some understanding of how you are doing, what you are doing, and how effective you are, but also should from time to time simply chat with you about the problems of your department. The middle manager and administrator should be interested in you and your family just as you are interested in your employees and their families. In fact, all human relations techniques that you utilize with your employees should be utilized with you by your middle manager and administrator.

There are certain techniques that should be used to sell your middle manager or administrator on your new ideas. They are as follows:

1. State precisely what the idea is in as simple terms as possible.

2. State the value of your idea to the organization.

3. Show the advantages and disadvantages of the idea.

4. Show how your idea fits into the overall operation.

5. Choose the right time and place to make the pitch.

6. Add your idea to some current program.

7. Suggest a trial run.

8. Have alternatives ready to discuss in case more information is wanted.

9. Make your presentation in capsule form.

10. Be prepared to present other supporting information.

XIII. SUMMARY

The "Fundamental Management Information" section discussed the function, responsibility, need for communications, and multiple roles of supervisors and managers.

This lesson has attempted to present some of the techniques of successful supervision and management. It has discussed supervisory problems, the use of time, education, how to make proper decisions, how to delegate authority, public relations, how to turn management policy into products and services, how to give instructions, get cooperation from employees, get ideas from employees, and how to get along with your middle manager or administrator. This lesson discussion, as in previous ones, is meant to be a building block on which each of the important areas of supervision and management can be placed in a proper sequence. By the time the two courses, Volume I and Volume II, are completed, each of the Fundamental Information Sections and the Lesson Discussion should fit into a total picture in a meaningful manner.

LESSON 3
CASE PROBLEM 1

Successful Supervisor

Bill Amish had been a district supervisor in the Walton County Health Department for 10 years. He supervised 17 professional employees. In the last few years he felt discouraged and his level of initiative had dropped substantially. He no longer obtained all of the necessary data before he made programmatic decisions. Three of his employees had become his buddies and therefore received the choice assignments. They were not held to the same standards as the rest of the staff. Bill was very critical in public concerning the work of four females on the staff. He felt that they were inadequate although they had the same training and education as the male members of the staff. They had children and therefore did not have the time to attend outside activities in the same manner as many of the male employees. One day, after he had received a call of complaint concerning Helen White, he immediately started to scream at her in front of the other staff members. He accused her of being lazy and not dealing with the public in an appropriate manner.

1. What qualities of supervision has Bill violated?

2. Did he use good judgment in singling out certain individuals for special attention?

3. Was he being fair in how he dealt with Helen White?

4. What would have been a better approach to dealing with Helen White?

5. What should he have based his decision on concerning quality and quantity of work?

ANSWER SHEET

LESSON 3
CASE PROBLEM 1

MANAGEMENT AND SUPERVISION FOR WORKING PROFESSIONALS

LESSON 3
CASE PROBLEM 2

Making Right Decisions

Jeff Broan was asked by his administrator, Sarah Fleet, to involve his staff in determining how to deal with an extended environmental emergency while maintaining crucial aspects of existing programs. Hurricanes in the past had disrupted the area and future ones were a certainty. Jeff asked Joan Cummings, one of his supervisors, to discuss the problem with the staff and present a plan of action to him within a week. Joan set up three groups of five staff members each and instructed them to develop a plan in three days and report back to her. Four weeks later Sarah Fleet asked Jeff if his report was ready. Jeff asked Joan, and Joan angerly demanded from the group leaders their report at once.

1. What did Jeff do wrong in making his assignment to Joan?

2. What did Joan do wrong in making her assignment to three group leaders?

3. Did Joan have a right to be angry with the group leaders?

4. How would you have utilized creative thinking to obtain the necessary ideas to deal with an extended emergency?

5. Once you had the employees' ideas what would you have done to arrive at the proper decision-making process?

6. What kind of a plan would you have developed related to maintenance of normal programs while servicing emergencies?

ANSWER SHEET

LESSON 3
CASE PROBLEM 2

MANAGEMENT AND SUPERVISION FOR WORKING PROFESSIONALS

PRACTICAL EXERCISES

You may do any two or more of these items.

1. For a one-week period carefully evaluate the amount of time you spend in each activity, how you establish your priorities, how you use your time, how you schedule your work, and how you delegate your responsibilities. This can be accomplished by writing down very briefly a response to each of these questions and then reading your responses at the end of the week.

2. Set up a chart by day, week, and month for a one-month period. On the chart list the day and date, and the time period broken down by fifteen- minute periods. The day and date should be at the top of the chart with the time periods running from top to bottom (8 a.m. to 5 p.m. or whatever is applicable). The first fifteen minutes of the day, plan on what you are going to do during the rest of the day. Then set forth each time period during that one-week period. Mention such things as opening and reading mail, handling phone calls, and giving workers instructions. At the end of the week, determine where your time has actually gone.

3. Using the previous information, set up a schedule of things you would like to do during the coming week. Write down the items and the amount of time that you would like to allocate to the items. Then, as in #2, write down the actual time spent carrying out your work. Determine what should be done to use your time more efficiently by working with the priorities which you have established.

4. Allocate your time by priorities during the course of the day. Try to stick to the schedule as much as possible. Where you find there are great difficulties in doing this, it may be necessary either to find a better way of delegating authority or you may have to change your priorities.

5. As a supervisor it is necessary to learn as much as possible. Therefore, develop a training program for yourself which is realistic. There are several suggestions in the Lesson Discussion on types of programs that you might want to follow. Remember, when your program is too rigid, you will not want to follow it. When it is interesting and only takes a limited amount of time you will achieve greater success. This is very similar to the individual who decides that he/she needs to exercise, runs five miles the first day, then is totally exhausted afterwards.

6. In order to make proper decisions, set down the major steps which are needed in decision making. The next time you

make a decision follow these steps in a chronological manner and evaluate the results and see if your decision-making process is starting to improve.

7. Determine who in your group can act as a supervisor. Then delegate the authority to this individual. Evaluate the person's performance, always keeping in mind that this person will not do as good a job as you would but still will get the work done in a satisfactory manner. Should the individual not fit the role well, then delegate the authority to someone else.

8. Determine how your company goes about handling public relations. Determine what you do as a supervisor to be part of this public relations program.

9. Evaluate employees who have to deal with the public by utilizing the list of six items mentioned in the Lesson Discussion. After you have completed your evaluation, discuss it with the employee in private. When he/she has done a very good job he/she should be commended. When he/she has done a poor job, try to strengthen weaknesses. When the public relations phase of the employee's work is mixed or average, commend the good portions, while offering suggestions to strengthen the areas where he/she is weak.

10. Determine whether or not you understand thoroughly your company's policies. Also, by questioning the employees, determine whether or not they understand company policy.

11. Give a set of instructions to your employees and then evaluate whether or not they understand the instructions by asking them, to repeat them to you and to show you how the work should be carried out. This should help you determine whether or not the instructions you give are clear and concise and given in a confident manner.

12. After you have given the previous instructions, determine whether or not you are meeting resistance. If you are, then use the techniques mentioned in the Lesson Discussion on how to get cooperation from employees.

13. Develop the concept of creative thinking among your employees. Do this by asking help and assistance from the employee. Use the techniques specified in the lesson discussion and determine whether or not they are applicable to your situation. Recognize that obtaining good ideas from employees is part of being a good supervisor. Therefore, you must improve yourself in this area. If the ideas start to increase and improve, then your job as a supervisor is getting better and stronger and you yourself are improving.

14. Evaluate whether or not you will sell your new ideas to the administrators. If you are not being too successful, apply the principles listed in the Lesson Discussion.

LESSON 3
PRACTICAL EXERCISES ANSWER SHEET

MANAGEMENT AND SUPERVISION FOR WORKING PROFESSIONALS

Do two exercises and number them. Use additional paper if necessary.

SELF-TESTING EXAMINATION #3

TRUE-FALSE QUESTIONS (CORRECT ANSWERS APPEAR ON PAGE 77)

1. A good supervisor is a planner, a source of technical knowledge, and a mediator. 1. __

2. The supervisor's major function is to transmit orders down to the subordinates. 2. __

3. Being a good listener is one of the most important roles of the supervisor. 3. __

4. Supervisors should transfer individuals, although they are doing a good job, to show who is in charge. 4. __

5. The supervisor's perks include coming and going as he or she desires. 5. __

6. The supervisor's different roles may cause a conflict. 6. __

7. Supervision includes selecting, interesting, teaching, and measuring people but does not include rating, commending, rewarding, or harmonizing. 7. __

8. A good supervisor controls and channels emotions rather than react to situations. 8. __

9. Unfortunately, new employees are taught how to assume time-killing routines. 9. __

10. Time is one of the key factors in a supervisor's success. 10. __

11. A means of managing time is to take a period of one hour each morning and determine what work should be done for the rest of the day. 11. __

12. When you delegate authority to someone you can expect them to do as good a job as you would have done. 12. __

13. When delegating authority you must accept the decisions and actions of individuals to whom you have delegated authority. 13. __

14. When delegating authority it is important to understand the capabilities of the person to whom you delegate the authority. 14. __

15. If your employee has a good personality you can assume that he/she can carry out good public relations.   15. __

16. It is important to keep individuals informed of company policy in order to keep the information "on the grape vine" reasonably correct.   16. __

17. It is essential to always check to see that an order is understood and that it is carried out. The individual who is receiving the order should be able to understand it the first time if he/she is competent.   17. __

18. Employees always cooperate with their supervisors, even if they have to do it grudgingly.   18. __

19. The best way to get an employee to cooperate is to look at your own good and bad qualities and thereby be sensitive to others' good and bad qualities.   19. __

20. Creative thinking is a function of management or supervision only.   20. __

21. Creative thinking is accomplished by sitting down, having meetings, and determining that this is the time to be creative.   21. __

22. By being a "yes man" you are pleasing to your boss and you obviously will be able to advance to a higher position.   22. __

ANSWERS TO LESSON 3 SELF-TESTING EXAMINATION

If your answer is incorrect, go back to the material referred to and determine why your answer is incorrect.

QUESTIONS FROM FUNDAMENTAL MANAGEMENT INFORMATION SECTION

1. T Beginning of Fundamental Management Information
2. F Beginning of Fundamental Management Information
3. T Middle of Fundamental Management Information
4. F Middle of Fundamental Management Information
5. F Middle of Fundamental Management Information
6. T End of Fundamental Management Information

QUESTIONS FROM THE LESSON DISCUSSION

7. F Beginning of the Lesson Discussion
8. T Beginning of the Lesson Discussion
9. T Beginning of the Lesson Discussion
10. T Beginning of the Lesson Discussion
11. F Beginning of the Lesson Discussion
12. F Beginning of the Lesson Discussion
13. T Middle of the Lesson Discussion
14. T Middle of the Lesson Discussion
15. F Middle of the Lesson Discussion
16. T Middle of the Lesson Discussion
17. F Middle of the Lesson Discussion
18. F Middle of the Lesson Discussion
19. T Middle of the Lesson Discussion
20. F End of the Lesson Discussion
21. F End of the Lesson Discussion
22. F End of the Lesson discussion

CASE PROBLEM 1 ANSWERS

Successful Supervisor

1. He made programmatic decisions without reviewing all necessary data. He made snap judgments based solely on his feelings. He became very friendly with three workers and gave them special treatment, which caused resentment among the other people. He was in fact sexually harassing the female employees, causing resentment, anger, and the possibility of a law suit. He harshly criticized an employee in front of other employees instead of discussing it with her in private.

2. NO! The other employees will become apathetic, angry, and resentful and the quality and quantity of work will decrease.

3. NO! A supervisor should never berate an employee. He should have investigated the incident and then tried to correct it in an effective and private manner. He humiliated her in front of her colleagues.

4. He should have called or spoken to other employees who may have information about the incident. He should have checked on the validity of the person making the complaint. He should have quietly asked Helen to see him in his office for a private discussion. At this time he should have told her about the complaint and asked her to tell her version. Then he should have made a decision in her favor or against her. If against, she should have been reprimanded in a professional manner following departmental policy.

5. He should have had measurable objectives based on the job descriptions and program plans. The individuals should have been trained to perform the work properly. The evaluation should have been based on the objectives related to quality and quantity of work performed.

CASE PROBLEM 2 ANSWERS

Making Right Decisions

1. Instead of Jeff Broan directing the emergency project and writing the report, he delegated this authority to Joan Cummings. He did not give her guidance and did not ask for the report in a specific time frame.

2. Joan Cummings in turn delegated to others without proper guidance and a time frame. She was bound to get three different plans, if the assignment would be carried out at all.

3. No, She did not have any right to be angry at them because she did not do her part as a leader. She should have set a due date for the reports to be in. If late, she should have investigated the reason for the delay. Above all, she was assuming that the individuals had the ability to carry out the assignment.

4. The group can create an emergency plan if they work together and share information. The group approach helps create ideas and suggestions which may stimulate others to think in a creative manner.

5. Evaluate all proposals and select the one which is best and most economically feasible. If all proposals contained some weak areas, select the strong points from each proposal and rewrite the plan.

6. Select supervisors who have had knowledge and experience in working with emergencies related to hurricanes. Brainstorm the problem to establish the necessary services and timetable to be used for emergency implementation. Divide the services among the supervisors according to their areas of expertise. Ask them to develop procedures, prepare a supply list, and name employees for their assigned areas, then report back in one week. These supervisors would be in charge of these services in the event of a real hurricane. During the week, prepare an emergency plan to staff existing programs with a minimal amount of people while freeing the remainder of the employees to assist in the disaster.

LESSON 4

PLANNING, ORGANIZING, AND BUDGETING

LEARNING OBJECTIVES

When you have successfully completed this lesson, you should:

1. Have learned the component parts of planning and organizing programs.

2. Have learned the proper steps necessary in carrying out a plan.

3. Understand how to make a plan acceptable and flexible.

4. Understand that deadlines and schedules are an extremely important part of the planning process.

5. Recognize that there are many techniques used for management, including management by objectives.

6. Have learned how to plan work schedules and the effect that planning has on you and your personnel.

7. Recognize the variety of time study techniques used and learn when to use them.

FUNDAMENTAL MANAGEMENT INFORMATION

INTRODUCTION

Planning is the process of determining what to do about a problem based on actual data which have been gathered. Budgeting is the process of providing the necessary dollars to operate the program and a means of controlling the program in a fiscally responsible manner.

STRATEGIC PLANNING

Strategic planning is the process of determining how to pursue the long- term goals of the organization with the resources which are expected to be available some five to ten years from now. Strategic planning is based on the strategies or general targets which the organization hopes to be pursuing in the future. It is in fact the general goals of the organization which will be accomplished within a certain time frame.The four major steps of strategic planning include: (1) formulating a master strategy; (2) formulating strategic plans; (3) implementing strategic plans; (4) strategic control. The master strategy answers the question of where is the organization going over time. Top management and planners define the purpose, direction, and priority of strategic goals. They are constantly reevaluating the strategic goals to determine if the priorities being established are realistic. Top management then formulates the strategic plans, policies, and budgets for reaching the strategic goals. Once again the

on-going evaluation helps them determine if the goals are realistic and if the budgets will be allotted by the various controlling groups to realize the goals. The implementation of the strategic plans is carried out based on top management's policies, budget constraints, and the middle and lower level managers' and supervisors' ability to formulate and implement operational plans. Again, on-going evaluation is needed to determine if what is being done is consistent and realistic. Finally, strategic control is based on information from all levels of supervision and management, which helps determine if progress is being made and also the kinds of problems being encountered. Note that evaluation is essential during all steps of this strategic process.

PLANNING

Planning is the process of preparing for change and coping with uncertainty by determining a future course of action based on the goals and values of the organization found in the strategic plan. Planning is a primary management function. Every act of management is intertwined with planning. Planning sets the stage for functions such as organizing, staffing, communicating, motivating, leading, and controlling. Planning is also needed to develop the appropriate budgets to carry out programs especially during times of limited resources and uncertain environments. When good plans are drawn, the chances of success are increased. The focus then is on the results of the

83

programs and not the mechanics of carrying out the activities. Planning forces individuals to evaluate appropriate data, determine alternatives, and arrive at decisions. Planning establishes a framework for decision making which is consistent with the goals and objectives developed by top management. Planning helps people become oriented toward an appropriate response to conditions rather than reacting to problems as they occur. Planning helps modify management's approach to problems, since the individual now has specific goals and objectives in mind and is focusing on them. Planning helps avoid crisis management and provides flexibility in decision making. Appropriate planning and measurable objectives are essential to improve not only program performance but also individual performance.

IMPLEMENTATION OF THE PLAN

In order to carry out any type of planning, including strategic planning, it is essential to have a good grasp of the problem the organization is facing; the demands placed on the organization by legislation from the federal and state levels; the type of organization and its structure; the number, attitude, age, and skill of its personnel; the technical performance and training of its personnel; and the amount of money available to carry out specific programs.

The strategic plan as well as any plan should have clear results-oriented objectives which are measurable and which have

specific time limits. The activities needed to accomplish these objectives and the responsibility and authority of individuals controlling these activities must be established. The level of resources available are important. Communications are essential for program plan implementation. Evaluation tells us what has happened.

FUTURISTIC FORECASTING

Futuristic forecasting is based on prediction, projections, or estimates of future events or conditions which will occur. Forecasting may be difficult since laws change and the public demands change. However the executive administrator must still try to look into the future and determine what needs will be in several years.

BUDGETS

Budgets are formally prepared financial projections which are needed in order to carry out specific programs for the organization. There are three types of budgets. The operating budget includes the projected revenues and projected expenses. The capital budget projects the source and uses of capital as well as the major outlays for buildings and possibly very expensive equipment. The financial budget keeps track of the cash flow and balance sheet as the programmatic areas proceed through the fiscal year.

ZERO-BASED BUDGETING

Zero-based budgeting is a means of operating and planning where the manager has to justify each detail of the budget and show proof of why the budgetary allotment should be made. Zero-based budgeting is a good idea because it forces the manager to take a hard look at what programs are being carried out, whether or not they are being successful, and the amount of people, equipment, and other resources which are committed to the given program.

It is much easier to submit the old budget along with an increase for inflation, then to go back and say, "Are we in fact doing what we should be doing in order to resolve the problems of today and the future." One problem with zero- based budgeting is that it is very time consuming and may occupy the time of individuals who are needed to handle problems that are currently occurring.

ROLE OF MANAGER AND SUPERVISOR

The middle manager and supervisor have a specific role in the planning process. It is their job to give input to higher management concerning problems and potential solutions. They then must take the program plan which has been developed at the higher levels and make it work. It is their job to determine how to schedule time, people, money, equipment, and materials in order to realize the measurable objectives which have been established. In order to do this they must define the objective or objectives to their subordinates. They must analyze the data which are available, develop the best plan and alternate plans, control the work as it is progressing, evaluate frequently, discuss and accept the critique, and accept suggestions and recommendations from the subordinates on how to better improve the process to make it work. One of the most important portions of the planning process for middle managers and supervisors is to establish proper time management. In order to do this, the manager or supervisor must be able to manage his or her own time effectively and understand how to develop a reasonable time schedule for subordinates. It is then up to a manager or supervisor to assist the subordinates in establishing a proper work load and work situation to carry out the program in an effective manner.

85

LESSON DISCUSSION

I. PLANNING AND ITS COMPONENT PARTS

The purpose of planning and the purpose of every plan is to help accomplish the objectives and goals of an organization. The planning is carried out by all managers, administrators, and supervisors. The efficiency of the plan is determined by what it contributes to carrying out the objectives and goals of the organization and how it does it in the least expensive and most efficient manner. Plans have five basic parts: objectives, policies, procedures, methods, and rules.

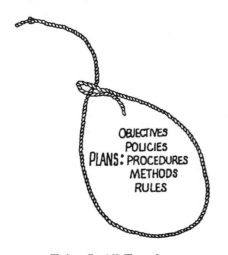

Tying It All Together

The purpose of the plan is spelled out clearly and concisely - then the objectives or goals are determined. In this way, there may be a concrete conclusion or result drawn from the work that is being done as the plan is carried out. When the meaning or the purpose is fuzzy, the objectives are fuzzy. When the purpose is clear, the objectives and goals are clear. The objectives must be of two types: the short-range objective, which can be realized very quickly and which will indicate that progress is being made toward the final goal, and long-range objectives, which take a longer period of time though in reality are the ultimate reason for carrying out the necessary work.

Since objectives are broad statements of what is wanted, it is necessary to set down a series of policies which serve as a guide in accomplishing the objectives. The policy is significant because it helps the employees move in the right direction toward achieving necessary objectives.

In order to put a policy into effect, a series of procedures or "how to go about it" items must be established. These are detailed steps describing precisely what should be done under a number of circumstances.

Since procedures may still be lacking in detail, the methods for accomplishing certain types of work are then set. Then the methods are taught to the individuals who will be carrying out the necessary work.

The rules are set to indicate boundaries by which the employees, supervisors, and others must live. The difficulty with rules is that they may become too restrictive. Perhaps they are poorly developed in the first place and therefore, have an improper effect upon the original plan. A good supervisor, if permitted, will make necessary changes in methods and rules as the occasion warrants.

Rules are plans of required action. They should not be confused with the policies or procedures. Remember that the policies are general statements which guide or channel thinking and action. Policies limit the area in which decisions should be made. Policies are made at several different levels and serve as basic guides. However, policies do leave a certain amount of discretion in carrying them out. Procedures are just a series of techniques used to handle the future activities. They are guides to action, not to thinking. Procedures can cut across departmental lines. The company policy can, for example, grant an employee a vacation, but the procedure establishes how the individual should schedule his/her vacation in order to avoid disrupting the work schedule. The rules require that a specific and definite action be taken. It is similar to the procedure in that it guides action but it does not specify a specific time. A procedure can almost be identified as a sequence of rules. For instance, 'no smoking' is a rule. However, the procedure involved in handling hazardous fire materials is a series of rules.

II. THE IMPORTANCE OF PLANNING

The four major goals of planning are to:

1. Set aside uncertainty and problems related to change.

2. Set up specific objectives.

3. Operate in an economical fashion.

4. Make control of the operation an easier task.

Nothing is more disruptive to an organization than uncertainty and change When the managers can see what is occurring, they will develop the necessary plans to account for changes in environment, society, markets, lifestyles, and so on. By careful thinking and then moving ahead effectively, the organization can continue to operate in a proper manner. With the plan comes the objectives. The objectives become concrete means for individuals to be able to move toward a very specific set of goals for the organization.

Planning reduces cost because you set up your efficient operation in advance. Thus, you have a consistent operation and you are able to avoid an uncoordinated group of activities. The work flows smoothly and the individual avoid considerable frustration.

The managers can control the organization because everyone in the organization is aware of the ultimate goals. Therefore, everyone is able to measure what is accomplished against what hopefully is to be accomplished.

III. PLANNING STEPS

The planning steps vary according to the types of program and the size of program. However, in any case, the planning steps should contain the following items: an awareness of change and the necessity for developing new programs and products. Establish objectives or goals to determine where the organization wants to go and where the primary emphasis should be placed. Based on these objectives and goals the strategies, policies, procedures, rules, budgets, and programs will be developed. Determine how the plans should operate. Set down the necessary alternatives. Evaluate the alternatives based on the goals you are trying to reach, the cost of the alternatives, and whether the alternatives are workable. Formulate the necessary plans for buying equipment, materials, and hiring and training employees. Develop the budgets necessary for all parts of the plan. Present the plan to the necessary organizations and individuals for approval. Modify the plan based on budget modification. Carry out the plan. Evaluate the results.

IV. MAKING A PLAN ACCEPTABLE AND FLEXIBLE

This can be accomplished by including key individuals, who might later object to the plan, in the planning process. It should also be recognized that new employees are much better able to change than older employees, and that all employees accept change better if they understand the reason for the changes and the values of the new program. Always make sure that the change is not perceived by the employees as a threat. You will notice that throughout the course emphasis has been on winning the support of employees rather then attempting to coerce them. It is difficult to make individuals do things they do not want to do unless you have a gun at their head. The employees will either make or break your new program.

Plans should be flexible. There should be room for improvement and change where necessary in order to arrive at the ultimate goal. Only during the actual work process can you determine if the plan is a workable one. At that time it will be necessary to modify, enlarge, decrease, change, or even possibly stop an operation because it is not moving forward as the plan was originally perceived. This means that there needs to be constant evaluation of what is occurring in order to determine if the plan is good and if it will reach the ultimate goals of the organization.

V. DEADLINES, SCHEDULES, AND TIME SPANS

Deadlines and schedules are an important part of the plan. It is necessary to determine how long the plan will take. Therefore, you will be able to say how much it will cost and how many people will be involved.

Deadlines and schedules also serve as a means of motivation. This gives individuals a particular time to work towards. The right time span varies with the kind of plan. If you are attempting to remodel your house, your time span might be 90 days. If you are attempting to improve and fix up your lawn and garden, your time span might be 30 days. However, if you are attempting to greatly reduce poverty in the United States, your time span may be 5-10 years. Therefore, it is essential that you do not allow either too little time, which is frustrating, or too much time, which tends to waste valuable materials and the efforts of people.

There are short-range plans and long-range plans which are utilized by management and supervisors. The short-range plan usually is part of a long-range program. The short-range plan may consist of building a series of roads into an area. The long-range plan may be to build shopping centers, hospitals, schools, homes, and an entire community. It is essential that the timing be proper and additional time be allowed for the uncertainties. Peculiar problems may arise in any given area.

VI. MANAGEMENT BY OBJECTIVES

Management by objectives, or MBO, is a process in which a group works toward achieving specific objectives and results as part of a larger organizational goal. Management by objectives is not necessarily a successful tool for all organizations. The organization must be sophisticated and must have the ability to plan, organize, direct, and control very carefully in order to operate in this manner.

In this technique the job content is designed around the results which are expected. All levels of the organization must participate in a cooperative manner and everyone on the staff is accountable for the results. If one group within the organization falls short of the expectations, it may lead to an imbalance. This will then cause problems in attempting to reach the final objectives.

VII. DECISION MAKING AND PLANNING

Once the plan has been established, certain people have to be designated to make the necessary decisions to carry out the plan. Since a plan cannot be very specific, it is up to the decision maker to move the plan along toward the ultimate objective. If the decision making is poor, the plan will fail no matter how good the plan was initially. Decision making can be based on data received from computers and on the impressions that supervisors or managers have on the operation.

VIII. PLANNING WORK SCHEDULES

The supervisors job is to get the work out. Although assistance is given in planning by a central scheduling department, it is the supervisor who must use his/her skill in planning to avoid waste in the department. The supervisor must be concerned with the following items:

1. Time - How can avoidable delays be prevented?

2. Materials - Will waste, spoilage, or unnecessary materials create delays or affect the operations?

3. Machines - Are they operating to their fullest capacity?

4. Space - Is there overcrowding, poor coordination of incoming supplies and outgoing work?

5. People - Are the employees occupied all the time?

6. Safety - Are situations such, that accidents will cause loss of time and also financial problems within the organization.

The supervisor should plan the amount and the type of work that should be done at least one week ahead of time. For some organizations, it is necessary to set up a monthly, weekly, and daily plan. If you find that you are too busy trying to resolve problems which are occurring all the time, you should stop and see if you are missing the opportunity to plan in advance and avoid these problems.

Good planning affects morale in a positive manner. Poor planning causes dissatisfaction, discouragement, anger,

indifference, and a variety of other problems. As a result of good planning, the individual can go home and realize that he/she accomplished what he/she set out to do during the course of the day. If you are constantly frustrated and unable to meet goals, your frustration may be demonstrated in a lackadaisical or angry attitude or in an increased level of accidents.

It is true that it takes time to plan. It takes time to sit down, jot down ideas, and put them in a systematic manner. However, if your road would be built without planning, it would meander through the countryside. It would go up the hills and across the rivers and continue to meander and perhaps it would never be completed. It is essential that the planning take place at not only the road-building level, but also at the construction crew level. This is where the supervisor determines precisely what should be done in each individual portion of the working week in order to accomplish objectives for that day and for that week.

It is important never to schedule at 100 percent of capacity. You should determine what the individuals can realistically do and make your schedule realistic.

Some of the problems you must anticipate when scheduling include:

1. Shift work. The individuals on shift work may not be able to adjust well to the late afternoon or night shifts and may, therefore, be inefficient. The attitude and training of the individuals is most important since many times

the immediate departmental supervisor is not present during the later shifts.

2. Recognize that speeding up the work beyond that which can be reasonably expected may cause a c c i d e n t s, t r e m e n d o u s dissatisfaction, discontent, and possibly even upheaval within the institution or company.

3. When you draw up your work schedules, you must account for holidays, vacations, rest periods, personal days, training time, absences, and other special situations.

IX. TIME STUDY METHODS

When a supervisor conducts a time study, he/she should first discuss it with the union, if a union exists, to make sure they understand that unreasonable work will not be expected of the employees. A supervisor, in conducting a time study, should not sacrifice quality for speed but should determine whether or not too much time is being utilized in carrying out certain types of tasks. A technique used for time study is to set up a chart listing each of the activities which a given job requires. Use standard symbols in the time study to represent each activity. The symbols might be a square for work time, a circle for preparation time, and a hexagon for transportation time. At the end of the day the evaluator will take a sheet and

determine precisely how much time is used in each of these activities. It should also be noted when and how individuals took coffee breaks at any given time and when and how individuals took lunch breaks at any given time. The purpose of this study is to find out where delays are occurring which interfere with efficiency. For instance, if the individual has to spend two hours in preparation time because the materials are not at hand and he/she must go to another building to obtain them, this accounts for two wasted hours. It might be a better process for a single messenger or a group of messengers or employees to distribute the materials and equipment at the job site in order to prevent this wastage of time. **Be careful. Do not antagonize the employees with the time study.** Discuss it with them and show them that what you are attempting to do is to obtain a better product or a better service. Point out that in the long run this study may even give them an increased salary. If they understand what you are doing and why you are doing it, the resistance to the study will be reduced considerably.

X. SUMMARY

The "Fundamental Management Information" section discussed planning, strategic planning, futuristic forecasting, budgets, zero-based budgeting, the role of the supervisor and manager in planning and decision making.

The Lesson Discussion has attempted to present the major components of planning, setting up schedules and deadlines, and developing proper time study techniques.

LESSON 4
CASE PROBLEM 1

Planning - A Way of Life

Susan Harper, the administrator of the York Nursing home, had just been visited by the State Health and Welfare Department team to determine if Medicare and Medicaid payments were being appropriately billed and if patients were receiving proper care. The team felt that the business office was not performing at an acceptable level. They felt that there were inadequate numbers of trained nurses to care for patients and that numerous instances of questionable medication and treatment were occurring. They felt that in the last several years no one had been concerned with futuristic planning and that the situation would worsen bringing about a possible cancellation of certification of Medicare and Medicaid benefits, which would result in the home closing.

1. What should Ms. Harper do about the existing problems in the business office?

2. What should Ms. Harper do about determining the level of patient care and improving it?

3. How should she deal with problems of medication and treatment?

4. What steps should she institute in order to plan appropriate work schedules and see to it that adequate professional supervision is available at all times?

5. What steps should be taken to anticipate future problems and develop appropriate plans to remedy them?

ANSWER SHEET

LESSON 4
CASE PROBLEM 1

MANAGEMENT AND SUPERVISION FOR WORKING PROFESSIONALS

LESSON 4
CASE PROBLEM 2

Budget Problems

Governor Andrews decided to freeze all positions in an attempt to balance the budget in this election year without raising taxes. John Stone, the public health administrator, lost numerous open positions in several divisions in the department and is operating with a diminished staff. Although programs must be carried out because of state and federal mandates, John called his division directors into a meeting and advised them of the governor's decision. He also stated that in his own review of the amount of work being produced he has found that the field personnel were spending approximately 50% of their time on field work. He stated that this would need to be improved drastically if mandated programs were going to be carried out. He asked that each of the division directors submit a plan of action to him in 2 weeks.

1. If you were a division director, how would you determine the proper time usage?

2. How would you utilize your people most effectively?

3. What expanded role would the secretarial staff carry out?

4. How should your field supervisors operate?

5. How would you establish appropriate deadlines, schedules and time spans?

Management and Supervision for Working Professionals

ANSWER SHEET

LESSON 4
CASE PROBLEM 2

MANAGEMENT AND SUPERVISION FOR WORKING PROFESSIONALS

PRACTICAL EXERCISES

You may do any two or more of these items.

1. Determine if your planning follows the eleven basic steps mentioned in the Lesson Discussion. The next plan which you are involved in should include these steps. Therefore, make a checklist and check off the items as you follow them in the planning process.

2. Determine if your plans are rigid or flexible, and what can be done to increase flexibility.

3. Determine if you establish realistic deadlines and set up realistic schedules. This can be accomplished by looking at a current plan and determining if the work is actually meeting the deadlines and schedules. If not, evaluate why not. The failure in the plan may be due to many things including improper scheduling.

4. Develop a work schedule utilizing the major items listed in the Lesson Discussion. Determine if the work schedule is effective and if the work is improving.

5. Develop a time study of the work being done by individuals you are supervising. If there is a union present, make sure that it is involved. The function of the time study should be to determine how time is used and what can be done to improve the work quality. Do this on a limited basis so that you can get some understanding of what is occurring but still will not antagonize the workers.

LESSON 4
PRACTICAL EXERCISES ANSWER SHEET

MANAGEMENT AND SUPERVISION FOR WORKING PROFESSIONALS

Do two exercises and number them. Use additional paper if necessary.

SELF-TESTING EXAMINATION #4

TRUE-FALSE QUESTIONS (CORRECT ANSWERS APPEAR ON PAGE 101)

1. Every act of planning is intertwined with management.　　　　1. __

2. Strategic planning discusses goals for 1-3 years in the future.　　2. __

3. The strategic plan should be results oriented.　　　　　　　3. __

4. The financial budget keeps track of cash flow.　　　　　　　4. __

5. Zero-based budgeting is always a good idea.　　　　　　　　5. __

6. Group decision making is the most effective technique of dealing with problems.　　　　6. __

7. The reason for planning is to provide the most effective techniques which can be used by an organization at the least cost.　　　　7. __

8. When planning, it is essential to spell out clearly and concisely the objectives or goals of the plan.　　　　8. __

9. Plans always contain short-range objectives, but rarely contain long-range objectives.　　　　9. __

10. The objective is a narrow statement of what is wanted. It is needed to set down a series of policies.　　　　10. __

11. Procedures may be lacking in detail but the methods for carrying out the procedures have to be spelled out.　　　　11. __

12. Rules are plans of required action.　　　　　　　　　　　12. __

13. Rules are the same as policies or procedures.　　　　　　　13. __

14. Planning helps reduce cost, and therefore makes an operation more effective.　　14. __

15. Although you may not necessarily stick strictly to a deadline or a schedule, it is important to establish deadlines when planning.　　　　15. __

16. Management by objectives is a technique which is highly successful in
    all organizations.   16. __

17. Because it takes time to plan, planning is not always the best use of time.   17. __

18. If you are going to be a good supervisor, you should schedule your programs at
    100 percent of capacity.   18. __

19. When scheduling for employees, you should consider such things as shift work,
    holidays, vacations, rest periods, personnel days, and so on.   19. __

20. A supervisor should conduct time studies. Time studies help reduce time
    wastage. A supervisor should assume that he/she has the right to carry out
    this type of supervisory function and should simply proceed to do so. 20. __

ANSWERS TO LESSON 4 SELF-TESTING EXAMINATION

If your answer is incorrect, go back to the material referred to and determine why your answer is incorrect.

QUESTIONS FROM FUNDAMENTAL MANAGEMENT INFORMATION SECTION

1. T   Beginning of Fundamental Management Information
2. F   Beginning of Fundamental Management Information
3. T   Middle of Fundamental Management Information
4. T   Middle of Fundamental Management Information
5. F   Middle of Fundamental Management Information
6. F   End of Fundamental Management Information

QUESTIONS FROM THE LESSON DISCUSSION

7. T   Beginning of the Lesson Discussion
8. T   Beginning of the Lesson Discussion
9. F   Beginning of the Lesson Discussion
10. F   Beginning of the Lesson Discussion
11. T   Beginning of the Lesson Discussion
12. T   Beginning of the Lesson Discussion
13. F   Beginning of the Lesson Discussion
14. T   Beginning of the Lesson Discussion
15. T   Beginning of the Lesson Discussion
16. F   Middle of the Lesson Discussion
17. F   Middle of the Lesson Discussion
18. F   Middle of the Lesson Discussion
19. T   Middle of the Lesson Discussion
20. F   Middle of the Lesson Discussion

CASE PROBLEM 1 ANSWERS

Planning - A Way of Life

1. Meet with the office manager and review all current procedures. Using the state guidelines, outline the proper Medicare and Medicaid filing procedures as well as proper record keeping. Ask the manager to meet with each of the employees, check their work procedures and where necessary change them. The manager should then report back findings. The question of possible fraud should be considered since typically an inaccurately completed form is rejected for payment.

2. The administrator, obviously, has not been doing her job if the quality of care has deteriorated to this point. She should visit (unannounced) each patient care area on all shifts and observe what is occurring. She should spot check several charts for documentation. She should meet the Director of Nursing to discuss the problems. The Director of Nursing should review all incidents and complaints, then determine the source of the problems. The Director of Nursing should provide data concerning current personnel levels and appropriate personnel levels to properly care for skilled, intermediate and residential classifications of patients. The Director of Nursing should provide recommendations for change in patient care.

3. Medication and treatment procedures should be discussed with the pharmacist, physical therapist, and nurses in charge of passing medications. Each should be asked to review all medication and treatment procedures. Each incident should be reviewed and discussed with the appropriate employees.

4. Using the state guidelines, Ms. Harper should evaluate the number of RNs and LPNs on each shift in proportion to the number of residents in each section. Employees should be reassigned to provide the necessary distribution of nurses and residents. Alternative personnel resources such as nurse placement agencies should be considered. Flextime may help resolve scheduling problems. Nurse competencies should be evaluated against goals and objectives.

5. A Quality Appraisal program should be implemented in each department to assure that quality service is provided, quality care is given, and proper procedures are followed. Ms. Harper should be visible in each department on a regular basis. She should meet with all department heads on a periodic basis to correct problems as they arise. Future problems could be anticipated by carefully evaluating all proposed rules and regulations at the state and federal level as soon as they are in the planning stages, and make appropriate changes

as they become effective. All assignments should be analyzed carefully and prioritized to provide and maintain excellent patient care.

CASE PROBLEM 2 ANSWERS

Budget Problems

1. Conduct a study of actual work being done in program areas by evaluating service time, office time, transportation time, and down time (including lunch and breaks). Find out through networking if other departments have better time usage, and determine if a better approach to satisfactory management is available. Evaluate how best to limit office time.

2. Develop schedules where individuals use minimal amounts of time in travel by grouping work activities in one area. Keep one professional in the office for two hours each day and allow others to rapidly leave for their field responsibilities. The secretaries should be able to reach field personnel through beepers or car radios. Where these are not available, personnel should call in the morning and evening. The supervisors should make sure that lunch hours and breaks are not abused.

3. The secretarial staff can answer many of the nontechnical questions and refer the technical ones to the professional in the office or other professionals when they are contacted during the day. The secretaries can help set up uniform letters on the computer, insert special sections, and help get them out rapidly.

4. The field supervisors should, on an ongoing basis, evaluate in the field the quality and quantity of work being performed and make necessary adjustments in a timely manner. Where several people have the same problem, training sessions should be set up for the staff. The supervisors should inform the managers of problems and potential solutions.

5. Deadlines, schedules, and time spans are based on the measurable objectives developed for the programs. They should be realistic. They should take into account what must be done and by what target date.

LESSON 5

EMPLOYEE SELECTION AND PEOPLE MANAGEMENT

LESSON OBJECTIVES

When you have successfully completed this lesson, you should:

1. Recognize that a part of the supervisors job is the improvement of work methods.

2. Realize that within the organization, there are formal groups, informal groups, and work groups. The supervisor should understand how to properly operate within these groups to achieve the objectives of the organization.

3. Recognize the need for good personnel management and the techniques utilized for employee selection which is the first part of personnel management.

4. Understand the necessity for special techniques in working with a new employee.

FUNDAMENTAL MANAGEMENT INFORMATION

INTRODUCTION

Human resource planning is the process of analyzing organizational needs for human resources under changing conditions and developing the specifications for the types of individuals who will meet these needs. The purpose of human resource planning is to obtain and retain the best qualified and most productive individuals for the organization. Retention is very important since it is costly to bring in people, train them, and then lose them to other situations.

RECRUITMENT OF PERSONNEL

The pool of potential employees may be obtained internally by posting jobs on bulletin boards and in the personnel office. This technique can be utilized especially for promotion from within. The pool of potential employees may be obtained from external sources as follows: 1) Advertising in newspapers or through executive search firms, 2) Utilizing computer management systems, 3) Contacting and placing ads in professional society journals or newsletters, 4) College recruitment, 5) The use of co-op and internship programs.

HIRING PROCESS

Legal Constraints - The legal constraints include: The Fair Employment Act of 1938; The Taft-Hartley Act of 1947; The Civil Rights Act of 1964; The Federal Age Discrimination in Employment Act of 1967, The Equal Pay Act of 1963; The Presidential Executive Order 11246 as amended by 11375 on prohibition against discrimination on the basis of race, color, religion, or national origin; The Vocational Rehabilitation Act of 1973; The Vietnam Era Veterans Readjustment Act of 1974; the state and local employment practices laws; the general law of the particular state, and the Americans with Disabilities Act of 1989. These laws will be explained in more detail in Volume II, Lesson 7 of the program, entitled "The Supervisor and Civil Rights."

Applications - The application process for new employees should follow these general guidelines: (1) Establish a clear and well written description of the job. (2) Treat all applicants fairly, equally, and consistently. (3) Establish a recruitment procedure manual with guidelines for various types of positions and follow the guidelines. (4) Check references before scheduling interviews for candidates. (5) Be aware of all conflicting laws and regulations governing the hiring process. (6) DO NOT VIOLATE THESE LAWS.

Interviews - The interview should be standardized. All candidates seeking the same job should be asked similar job- related questions. The interviewer should ask about relevant job skills, knowledge, accomplishments, and reasons for leaving previous positions. The interviewer should determine what the person has done in previous job experiences that are related to the new job. Utilize only the job- related educational experience of the applicant.

Once the individual has been pre-selected by the personnel department, including the initial interview, completion of all necessary forms, and the checking of references and registrations, the individual should then be sent to the supervisor who will make the final decision on the hiring. The supervisor should have complete knowledge of the recommendations of individuals who have been used as references by the person applying for the position. The supervisor should discuss, in a very direct manner, the various facets of the job and the goals and objectives set forth as well as the expectations of the organization. The supervisor should read the application forms carefully, check all examination scores and any other pertinent information prior to the time that the applicant arrives for this most essential interview. When conducting the interview the supervisor or manager should first put the applicant at ease, stick to a planned schedule, listen attentively, remain neutral, and make an honest decision concerning the applicant's ability to handle the job and work with the work group. It is important that the supervisor not use the "halo effect" in choosing an applicant for employment. This amounts to personal bias and should never be part of an interview process. The "halo effect" could mean that someone is particularly good looking or the individual may have clothes, cosmetics, earrings, etc.,

which are personally repugnant to the interviewer. Acceptable questions include the academic and professional background, work experience, participation in professional organizations, references, reasons for wanting to be employed with the organization, and goals for the future.

Always be aware of the fact that you must not discriminate against minorities. In some agencies or corporations there is an affirmative action policy which states that if people are basically of the same quality through education and experience the agency should make an attempt to hire a minority for the position.

An applicant should not be kept waiting for long periods of time to hear whether or not he or she has been chosen for a position. If the individual is not chosen, it should be for the following appropriate reasons. (1) No previous or insufficient job experience. (2) Lack of necessary qualification. (3) More qualified candidates exist. (4) Bad references. (5) Applicant lied on the application. (6) The individual rejected the offer.

It is essential that you do not reject candidates because they are married women, pregnant, unwed mothers, or have preschool-age children. Training opportunities that are presented to white males must also be presented to minorities and women. You must not decide that women or minorities cannot handle certain jobs because of the preference of the community or directors of the programs.

ORIENTATION AND TRAINING

All employees need to complete a general orientation to the institution and specific training to develop necessary competencies to meet the job skills required for the position. The time allotted for these activities should be long enough to familiarize the individual, but short enough to be cost effective. (see the supervisor as a teacher, discussed in Volume II, Lesson 3).

DEVELOPMENT

Development is part of human resource planning. Development is the process of promoting the personal growth of the individual to help prepare for better positions in the organization. Individuals who are hired by an organization want to advance. They must first meet the basic specifications of the job and then have the ability to learn and mature in the working environment. They must exhibit technical professional skills along with continuing enthusiasm. Then career development occurs through guidance counseling and the provision by the organization for specific types of additional training to enhance their skills.

CONTROLS

Controls are the techniques used to make something work. They are techniques used to try to correct problems and to get individuals to carry out their job in an adequate manner. The five major characteristics of control include being timely, appropriate, adequate, understandable, and economical. A control is a way of making something happen the way it should happen. Controlling is the process that supervisors and managers go through to control individuals and situations. Control of a situation or individual is based on measuring performance, comparing measured performance to standards and taking appropriate corrective action.

PERFORMANCE MEASUREMENT

Before managers can determine what must be done to make the organization more effective or efficient they must measure performance. Performance must be based on measurable objectives. Measurable objectives must be established by individuals who are technically and administratively qualified to understand the program area. Before you can measure you must establish a standard of activity which involves quantity and quality of work. These standards must be reasonable. Where individuals do not meet the standards the supervisor must determine why this is occurring, what problems need to be eliminated, and if the individual needs retraining or further training. Once retraining or further training and resolving of problems has occurred and the performance standards are still not met, it may be necessary to start the process of corrective action. The topic of evaluation of personnel will be discussed in Volume II, Lesson 6 under the performance ratings.

CORRECTIVE ACTION

Corrective action is discussed in Volume II, Lesson 4 under disciplinary action, complaints, and grievances. The ultimate result of improper corrective action may be a grievance.

Before the supervisor or manager starts any type of corrective action the individual must understand what potential barriers exist for the successful completion of the task. The barriers may include the following: (1) Pushing individuals to do more work than is reasonably possible. (2) Increasing employees' frustrations with their jobs and reducing morale by constantly changing requirements for the task. (3) Encouraging the falsification of reports in order to meet goals and objectives which cannot be met.

At times the amount of work needed to be done is so overwhelming that the individual cannot possibly carry it out. The supervisor or manager should do a quick evaluation of the job and establish priorities for the individual in order to avoid frustration and to promote the accomplishment of major tasks and the allowance of minor tasks to be done at a future date.

SUMMARY

Human resource planning includes proper recruitment, hiring, training, developing of skills, providing opportunities for growth, and advancement. Making the

program work includes use of time and appropriate control, performance measurement, retraining, and when necessary positive corrective action.

LESSON DISCUSSION

I. IMPROVING WORK METHODS

Improving work methods will lower cost of products and services and, in general, produce higher quality services and products. This can be accomplished by looking at the job, subdividing it into tasks and subtasks, and determining how long as well as how much each portion of the job takes to complete. The good supervisor not only carries out this evaluation frequently, but also asks employees how the job can be done in a better and more comfortable manner. The best technique is to take one of the simple tasks carried out by an employee and break this task into its smallest component parts. Check each step along the way to make sure that you have covered all the parts and to make sure that you can determine where any delays may occur. By simply reducing the delays you may be able to save time and, therefore, have a better and less expensive product. It is a good idea to develop a flow chart where you indicate how a process or job flows from the beginning to the end service or product. This flow chart should be shown to the employees and they should be permitted to add any details which are necessary to clarify the diagram. The diagram should be truly representative of the actual work being done. Time periods of the represented work should be assigned to each appropriate section on the flow chart. Then, a team of employees who are best suited to do this particular job should follow these steps through as indicated on the chart. It should be determined how long it took to complete the process and whether any special problems occurred. As problems and delays are found, once again they should be corrected and the flow chart modified until it finally represents the actual work of the group doing the work.

II. FORMAL ORGANIZATIONS

The formal organization is established by the company to accomplish specific goals and tasks. People form these organizations because:

1. They feel they will be more effective as a group or unit.

2. They can better provide for some of their wants and needs by forming a group.

3. This group will provide the members with a sense of security and a means for defending themselves.

4. It allows for socializing.

The formal organization has a specific hierarchy which establishes policies, procedures, methods, and rules. They enforce these norms by use of rewards and penalties. They establish rituals, symbols, dress and behavior codes, and so on. The formal organization (an example of which would be the U.S. Department of Health and Human

Services) has a series of very well-defined goals and objectives which the employees work toward achieving.

III. INFORMAL ORGANIZATIONS

Informal organizations occur spontaneously. They may arise to satisfy a particular need and then disappear when the need has been fulfilled. If a traffic light was needed at the intersection near a school, a group of parents might form an informal organization to bring pressure on the authorities to get a traffic light installed. Once the light had been installed, the purpose of the organization would cease to exist and the organization would probably disband. The informal group has its own communication system, standards, rules, and regulations. The foremost functions of the informal organization are to:

1. Satisfy social needs.

2. Satisfy the various needs of communication.

3. Set up and maintain standards of work and conduct.

4. Contribute to the accomplishments which result in high-quality work produced in quantities.

Informal organizations as well as informal power structures may have tremendous influence on the employees to achieve or resist work. They have their own grapevines, their own social groups, cliques, and so on. The grapevine should be plugged into a legitimate source of information. This will enable inconsistencies and errors in information to be corrected and proper information to be fed into the group.

The supervisor must learn how to work with the informal groups, evaluate group attitudes and morals, and keep from threatening the group or having the group threaten the supervisor.

IV. WORK GROUPS

Work groups are informal groups organized by individuals who work in the same profession or occupation, or simply work at the same location. The work group establishes its own hierarchy of relationships based on influence, positions held, leadership traits, and communication skills. These groups usually have a common set of desires. They may try to do the following:

1. Fill a need for positive social interaction.

2. Provide for the control of group actions.

3. Exercise substantial influence over the work environment.

4. Enhance the effectiveness of the group vs. the effectiveness of a single individual.

A group may have a broad range of views although they have a common purpose. They usually receive some direction from the formal power structure. The work group will constantly change in size and in make-up depending on the needs of the formal structure.

A work group should have: a clear idea of the direction in which they are heading, a flexible schedule, a clear communications process, the ability to achieve objectives, the ability to use leadership, cohesiveness, and the ability to adjust to the environment.

V. MANAGEMENT OF PEOPLE

Management of people is the proper and useful technique of using your employees to accomplish the best quantity and quality work. Where inefficient management of people exists the following may occur:

1. High employment turnover rate.

2. Excessive absences and lateness.

3. Many grievances.

4. Poor quality work.

5. Low quantity of work.

It takes a substantial amount of money, well beyond the actual salary an individual is paid, to employ an individual on a yearly basis. It cost more money to hire a new employee than to keep an employee who has been with the company several years. The new employee must be trained, and during the training period the new employee is of very little value from a productive point of view. The supervisor has to understand all of these concerns about people and has to be able to negotiate with these individuals in such away to get the best possible job out of each person. This will be discussed in later sections of this course.

In some areas there may be over-staffing and in other areas understaffing. The amount of staff should be based on the amount of work which must be carried out. The staffing should be very realistic.

VI. OFFICE MANAGEMENT

The organization operates most efficiently if it has a good office manager, secretary, and a proper filing system. There must be good coordination between the professionals, other employees, and the clerical staff. Each group should have an understanding of how each unit fits into a specific role and must understand that the final results are achieving the goals of the organization. The office should have good lighting, proper ventilation, air conditioning, and should be roomy enough for all individuals to work in a compatible manner. The secretaries play an enormous role in the operation of the organization since they are involved in scheduling of meetings and appointments. They are public relations specialists since they provide the first impression for the institution or company.

They move the necessary paper and perform the necessary computer operations in an accurate and rapid manner. This enables the decisions made by top management to be spread to all levels of management and then be put into operation.

Individuals should attempt to cut down on paperwork whenever possible. We spend too much time doing paperwork and not enough time actually carrying out our service concerns. Since it is impractical to totally do away with special paperwork, the special paperwork should be saved for emergency problems or for a time when the office is not functioning as it usually does.

Forms are an excellent means of standardizing inspections, surveys, studies and necessary data gathering in a variety of areas. However, we can have too many forms, and we can keep them around too long. It is necessary to have a group of individuals carry out forms control evaluation, so that limited numbers are produced and less storage space is needed for the forms from prior years.

Some steps which should be followed in order to get a better filing system are to:

1. Decide which information is useful and which should be thrown away.

2. Decide how often you need this kind of information.

3. Keep the paper if it is a summary of other reports.

4. Ask if this information could be duplicated from other sources quickly if it were lost.

5. Ask if the reports are needed to meet either financial statements or government regulations such as those of OSHA, EPA, or Department of Health and Human Services.

6. Check to see if the documents are being retained for legal purposes.

7. Ask how important this information is to other individuals.

8. Ask how long should the information be kept on file.

9. If the information is on the computer, is the computer secure.

Work simplification in the office is similar to work simplification in the institution or plant. In-depth evaluations must be made, competencies determined, and jobs must be divided into their simplest steps. After the evaluations, you will be able to determine the areas of delays and areas of problems. You should then be able to improve your operation. It is important to recognize when individuals are doing too little work, too much work, and when they are passing up the opportunities to improve their work. Should better equipment or better materials be provided for them? Office machinery should be modern, easily usable, and easily serviced. Copying machines should be modern and used solely for business purposes.

Personal calls will be made by individuals in the office no matter what you do. However, the wise supervisor will see that employees are not charged for local calls or for long-distance calls made in an emergency. On the other hand, workers should fully realize that the institution or company is operating for the purpose of producing a specific product or service and extended personal calls or a large number of personal calls should not be permitted.

Unfortunately, there is a considerable amount of purse stealing, equipment stealing, and other types of thievery going on in offices. Office personnel and others should be alerted to these problems. Steps should be taken to
protect their personal belongings and the belongings of the company.

In most office situations, coffee breaks are permitted. It is wise to schedule the coffee breaks and lunch breaks in such away that the phones are always covered and the work of the organization continues during breaks.

VII. EMPLOYEE SELECTION

Employee selection is carried out initially through the personnel office by means of examinations, interviews, searches of backgrounds, evaluation of references, past experience, and so on. The supervisor becomes involved in the selection process by interviewing the potential candidate for his/her department. The interview is an important part of determining whether or

not the employee has the personality and the willingness to work effectively within a specific department of the organization.

Employee Selection

The supervisor should be careful in the interview process to secure whatever information is needed to better understand the candidate. The supervisor must give information concerning the job as well as provide answers to questions concerning policies and procedures. It must be determined if the applicant matches the position requirements. During the interview the supervisor should carry out the following steps:

- Exhibit a positive attitude and interest in the future employee.

- Ask the individual about previous jobs he/she held and why he/she left.

- Attempt to remove personal biases and prejudices in the interview.

- Put the individual being interviewed at ease.

- Understand the job, type of individual that should be filling the job, and determine if the person being interviewed will match the requirements.

- Use language that is easily understood.

- Listen intently for all types of information which may be offered. It is important to get the individual to talk and to present his or her ideas and other necessary information.

The supervisor should avoid:

- Spending too much time getting down to the business of the interview.

- Using the individual's appearance as an indication of the ability to carry out the job.

- Making snap decisions.

- Badgering the individual.

- Arguing with the individual.

The supervisor is given a unique opportunity in the interview process of making the judgment concerning the potential employee. If the supervisor does not feel confident in making these types of judgments, help should be sought and additional training from management should be necessary.

VIII. THE EMPLOYEE'S FIRST DAYS

The employee's first days and probably first week are the most important time periods in his/her work life. During this period of time the employee is developing habits as well as an outlook concerning the job, people around him/her, and the organization at large. It is at this time the supervisor must spend considerable time training, coaching, and leading the new worker. The new employee must start with a good impression and it is up to the supervisor to make this impression. At times, because of the amount of work the supervisor has to do, the job of orienting the new worker is given to one of the subordinates. If this is done, it is essential to select a subordinate who is a good teacher, a friendly individual, and who demonstrates enthusiasm for work. At this time, it is necessary to encourage the individual to talk about himself/herself, his/her interests, and what the individual hopes to achieve in his/her work as well as what he/she wants from life.

Make sure that the new employee has a personal desk or place to carry out work. The new employee should also know where to find the lockers, washroom, lunchrooms, infirmary, and so on. It is also helpful to

116

have a formal orientation period of a day or more concerning the operation of the total organization as well as where he/she fits into the organization. Time should be spent on teaching the employee how to carry out assigned work and how to perform the work in an efficient and effective manner. The employee should have an understanding of personnel policy. A good way of handling this is to present the employee with a booklet, in simplified terms, which spells out the personnel policy of the organization including such things as medical care, insurance policies, leaves, promotions, and discipline.

During the early stage of the individual's work, he/she should be encouraged to ask many questions. During the first few days the supervisor must never show irritation toward the new employee because of asking questions or making mistakes. This is, of course, the time when the employee will be making the greatest number of mistakes and the time when he/she needs to learn what is expected. There are many questions which an individual will ask a supervisor. Some typical ones are:

- How long is the probation period?

- What is my title?

- How do I report an absence?

- Are there any policies concerning layoffs?

- When is lunch period and how long are coffee breaks?

- Is smoking permitted?

- Must I join a union?

- When is payday?

- Do I get special pay for special time periods?

- May I take off religious holidays?

- Do I get pay for attending National Guard camp?

- How long is vacation?

- Do we earn bonuses?

- How are raises given?

- Are there any tuition refund programs?

- What kind of fringe benefits do I receive?

- Is there a credit union?

- Are there company clubs, bowling, etc.?

- Can I get discounts when I purchase company made products or use institutional services?

- Are there any company or institutional newspapers?

117

- How do I participate in activities which help me to advance?

IX. SUMMARY

The Fundamental Management Information section discussed human resource planning, career development, legal constraints, job posting, the application process, the interview process, selection discrimination, performance expectations, and initial employee evaluation.

The lesson discusses how to improve work methods, the differences and importance of formal and informal organization(including work groups), proper people management as well as office management, employee selection, and how to properly orient new employees.

LESSON 5
CASE PROBLEM 1

Management of People

Jill Collins, the City Manager, was very concerned about the Westford Wastewater Treatment Plant. The operation of the plant was haphazard and had been cited by the State EPA. There was a high level of employee turnover. There were excessive absences and lateness and grievances in the last three months. Obviously, the quantity and quality of work was poor. It appeared that the secretarial staff was constantly swamped by paper work and were so disgruntled that numerous complaints were being made by the public.

1. What would you do about determining the problems at the plant?

2. Why did Jill Collins wait until so many problems occurred?

3. How would you deal with employee turnover, absenteeism, and lateness?

4. How would you create an efficient office system?

5. Who is at fault initially?

6. Who is at fault eventually?

ANSWER SHEET

LESSON 5
CASE PROBLEM 1

MANAGEMENT AND SUPERVISION FOR WORKING PROFESSIONALS

LESSON 5
CASE PROBLEM 2

Employee Selection

Albert White, the departmental supervisor, was resentful because his ideas had not been used by his boss, Dr. Jones. While interviewing new college graduates for a position in his department he was very impatient. He particularly did not react well to the Hispanic, Jose Gonzoles. He felt that they were overrunning the city and taking jobs away from other people. Lucy Pitts was overdressed and wore to much makeup and Harold Stiles appeared to be effeminate. He proceeded to badger Gonzoles, Pitts, and Stiles. He finally hired Joe Smith, a friend of a friend.

1. What mistakes did Albert White make in the interview process?

2. Did he break any laws?

3. How would you select a new employee? What would you look for?

4. Did Dr. Jones make any errors by not accepting Mr. White's ideas?

ANSWER SHEET

LESSON 5
CASE PROBLEM 2

MANAGEMENT AND SUPERVISION FOR WORKING PROFESSIONALS

PRACTICAL EXERCISES

You may do any two or more of these items.

1. Evaluate the work process step-by-step for each work area. Determine how the tasks are being accomplished and how they can be improved.

2. Determine what comprises the informal organizations within your company and how they affect the work which is being done.

3. Determine if the work groups follow the suggested principles necessary for a good work group.

4. Evaluate the work carried out in an office and determine if it is being effectively completed.

5. Based on the principles defined in employee selection, determine if you utilize these principles in the next interview you have with a potential employee.

LESSON 5
PRACTICAL EXERCISES ANSWER SHEET

MANAGEMENT AND SUPERVISION FOR WORKING PROFESSIONALS

Do two exercises and number them. Use additional paper if necessary.

SELF-TESTING EXAMINATION #5

TRUE-FALSE QUESTIONS (CORRECT ANSWERS ON PAGE 126)

1. The purpose of human resource planning is to hire and retain the best person.   1. __

2. The Equal Pay Act of 1990 makes equal pay for equal work mandatory.   2. __

3. The interview conducted by the department manager is most essential.   3. __

4. You can reject a pregnant woman, if you think it is a poor job for her.   4. __

5. Measurement of individual performance is based on your experience.   5. __

6. Employees should perform at the rapid levels you establish.   6. __

7. The development of the flow chart of a process is important since it allows you to determine where the slowdowns occur.   7. __

8. The informal power structure is not accepted within the organization since it is a nuisance to the organization.   8. __

9. The work group is static and, therefore, does not change in size and make-up.   9. __

10. A good organization operates effectively when it has a good, efficient office manager, good secretarial help, and proper office procedures.   10. __

11. Forms are used as a means of standardizing inspections and studies. However, we tend to have too many forms and we tend to keep them too long.   11. __

12. Work simplification in the office is totally different from work simplification in the plant since one is a white-collar job and the other is a blue-collar job.   12. __

13. Coffee breaks, although taken, are not permitted by law.   13. __

ANSWERS TO LESSON 5 SELF-TESTING EXAMINATION

If your answer is incorrect, go back to the material referred to and determine why your answer is incorrect.

QUESTIONS FROM FUNDAMENTAL MANAGEMENT INFORMATION SECTION

1. T Beginning of Fundamental Management Information
2. F Beginning of Fundamental Management Information
3. T Middle of Fundamental Management Information
4. F Middle of Fundamental Management Information
5. F End of Fundamental Management Information
6. F End of Fundamental Management Information

QUESTIONS FROM THE LESSON DISCUSSION

7. T Middle of Lesson Discussion
8. F Middle of Lesson Discussion
9. F Middle of Lesson Discussion
10. T Middle of Lesson Discussion
11. T Middle of Lesson Discussion
12. F Middle of Lesson Discussion
13. F Middle of Lesson Discussion

CASE PROBLEM 1 ANSWERS

Management of People

1. Meet with supervisors to identify specific problems. Review the EPA criticisms. Determine the source of the problems and possible solutions.

2. Jill Collins, after selecting the plant manager, assumed that he would operate in an appropriate manner. She never really determined if he had proper supervisory skills to accomplish the job, initiative to deal with problems, and the ability to analyze the reason for the problems as they occurred. She did not require an appropriate timely report to keep her aware of what was going on.

3. To deal with employee turnover, absenteeism, and lateness, find out why they are occurring, analyze the data, determine the workable solution and alternatives, and take necessary action. Absenteeism and lateness should be dealt with by the supervisor in a private conference with the individual. Violations should be corrected in a given time period. Follow-up and use of additional action as needed, including termination, may be necessary if the employee will not correct the situation.

4. Review work assignments of each office person as well as the description of the job. Identify inadequacies requiring change. Plan work assignments. Provide necessary equipment and training. Hire a competent office manager.

5. The Plant Manager.

6. The City Manager.

CASE PROBLEM 2 ANSWERS

Employee Selection

1. Albert White allowed his resentment toward his supervisor to dictate his behavior during the interviews. He allowed his personal prejudices to interfere with the interview process, rather than look at the candidates' qualities, experience, and potential to fill the position. He badgered the individuals.

2. He apparently broke the affirmative action and discrimination laws by his approach to the individuals. This may be hard to prove, since nothing was in writing.

3. Employee selection should include: review of resumes, personal interviews, questions regarding experience and abilities; describing position, goals and objectives; and allowing candidates to offer his/her opinion of ability to carry out the job. Ask the candidate to describe strengths and weaknesses by means of explaining credentials, experience, and education. Evaluate references and verify them.

4. Dr. Jones should have encouraged ideas from a subordinate. He could always ask the individual to further develop the idea and resubmit it to him. If the idea was not feasible, at least the individual would know that the administrator was interested.

LESSON 6

UNDERSTANDING HUMAN BEHAVIOR

LEARNING OBJECTIVES

When you have successfully completed this lesson, you should:

1. Understand that we as individuals as well as our employees and supervisors act and react in a variety of ways because of many different reasons.

2. Recognize some of the factors which control our behavior.

3. Recognize the need for good human relations and some of the techniques which are used to achieve good human relations.

4. Understand the process of group dynamics and how best to work within the group.

5. Recognize the role of trust and confidence in the working environment and how to achieve this with our employees.

6. Understand the types of things which cause people to be motivated and how best to motivate them in a manner which is healthy for the individual as well as the organization.

FUNDAMENTAL MANAGEMENT INFORMATION

INTRODUCTION - HUMAN NEEDS

There are five basic human needs: physical, safety and security, social, esteem, and self realization. Physical needs include food, clothing, shelter, and survival. Safety needs include physical security and prevention of accident and injuries which cause loss of jobs and loss of the ability to function in a satisfactory manner. Social needs include human companionship, affiliation with individuals and groups, a sense of identity, being with people who care and are concerned. The need for esteem includes being respected by others and having a good self image. The need for self realization includes the ability to fulfill our potential and creativity.

SUPERVISOR'S ROLE

The supervisor and manager have to be aware of human needs in order to be able to carry forth the proper role assigned to supervision. It is the supervisor who helps provide the physical needs by employing the individual which results in financial stability. The supervisor is prominently involved in safety and security. The supervisor should recognize the individual's need for socialization, esteem, and self-realization and try to satisfy them during the course of employment. Recognition of unsatisfied needs is the first step toward a better employee relationship. The supervisor accomplishes this through discussion and

counseling, by observing actual working conditions, by giving adequate training, and finally by giving recognition when due. The supervisor should know: 1) What are the employee's immediate goals? 2) What are the employee's immediate needs? 3) What are his or her unique attitudes about the supervisor, job and company? 4) Why does the employee hold these attitudes? This information is vital.

FRUSTRATION

Everyone, the president of the company or the newest hired employee, experiences frustration in his or her job. Frustration in small amounts can be a motivating factor and can cause the individual to work harder to achieve goals. Frustration in larger amounts can be defeating and cause the individual to give up or become involved in an accident. It is up to the supervisor to make sure that the level of frustration does not reach a serious point.

STRESS

Job Related - Frustration can lead to stress. Stress is a nonspecific physiological response to anything that challenges the body. Stress may be related to the conditions around us that are causing a feeling of discomfort or strain. It may also be applied to the internal reaction we have to these stressors from the external environment. Stress can eventually lead to burnout, which then can lead to an individual who is either unable to cope with his or her job or is now doing it poorly. Some jobs are more stressful than others. For instance, air traffic controllers certainly are under far greater stress than the individual who is coordinating the efforts of building a highway. Although the latter job is stressful, the individual is not faced with the possibility of many people immediately dying as a result of a miscalculation.

Stress reactions may be due to the boredom of watching various electronic devices or sources of information, making decisions, performing certain specific activities, being in a hazardous job situation, being in a stressful environment, and constantly working with people. Stress may be due to too little work or too much work. The person with too little work may be overtrained, lack job variety, be bored with the assignment, and have a sense of accomplishing little or nothing of value. The person with too much work may be stressed because of too much responsibility, inadequate training, inadequate time to complete the work, feelings of being overwhelmed, or working at too rapid a pace. Some individuals are stressed because of conflicting demands made upon them. When an individual works extremely well at a technical job and then is promoted to supervisor, the individual now faces the need to maintain the same level of job competency plus all of the responsibilities related to management. This can result in both quantitative overload and qualitative overload. In quantitative overload the person is simply physically unable to keep up with the activities. In qualitative overload the person feels that he or she lacks the skill or abilities required to adequately perform a given job. Many times, people feel that the responsibility for others is very burdensome. These individuals may start to develop the physical symptoms of stress such as ulcers, hypertension, nervousness, pain, and inattentiveness. When an individual is not allowed to participate in making decisions this person feels helpless and feels as if his/her life is out of control. This certainly contributes to a stressful situation.

Outside Factors - People also have outside factors which contribute to the stress of their job. They may be sick, they may have sick children or family members, have money problems, or be involved in a large number of other events such as death of a spouse, divorce, separation, personal injury or illness, trouble with the law, change in sleeping habits, change in eating habits, or involved with chemical dependency.

Health Effects - Stress not only affects health: stress may kill. Response to stress includes an increase in heart rate, muscle tension, blood pressure, blood sugar, blood cholesterol, and blood coagulability. Physical disfunction may result. Physical ailments include coronary heart disease, hypertension, obesity, diabetes, asthma, tension headaches, migraine headaches, ulcers, cancer, and a greater susceptibility to infectious diseases and accidents. Stress may also cause a variety of emotional disorders and mental illness.

Underlying Causes - Part of stress is based on behavior and behavior may be very difficult to alter. Part of stress may be based on the needs and wants of an individual that cannot be satisfied. Needs are those things that the individual desires to achieve or have. Part of stress may be based on the individual and his or her culture. Part of stress may be based on poor supervision or management. Part of stress may be based on attitudes. In any case, these stressful situations, as indicated previously, can be extremely hazardous to the individual's health.

MOTIVATION

Motivation is an individual's inner state that causes him or her to behave in a way that insures that he or she will accomplish some goal. Motivation is the drive that an individual uses to achieve that personal goal. Motivation explains why people behave the way they do. A person who is motivated feels that he or she needs to accomplish something. This type of individual is continually setting goals to meet new wants and once these are satisfied again sets new goals to meet new wants. Not only is it necessary to motivate someone, but once motivated, the individual must maintain the level of motivation. This can be accomplished by presenting challenging work, a feeling of personal accomplishment, recognition for achievement, granting increasing responsibility, giving a sense of the individual's importance, providing necessary information, and involving the person in the decision-making process.

Management Strategies - Good motivation can also be created by providing adequate training, autonomy, opportunity for advancement, personal time, adequate salary, good working conditions, and most important of all, good supervision and management. A good supervisor satisfies intrinsic needs such as additional salary, commendations, extra leave time, and other types of recognition.

Some other motivational strategies include job rotation, job enhancement, job enrichment, flex time, and behavior modification, which is brought about by positive reinforcement when things are done in a good manner.

Group Behavior - Human behavior is tied to the group on many occasions, and needs and wants can be satisfied by the group. Motivation may also be reinforced through the group. It is essential to understand how the group works and why it does what it does. A group is composed of two or more people who are aware of one another, who consider themselves to be a functioning unit, and who are trying to achieve a specific goal or goals. Group dynamics is made up of forces which come from: 1) The individuals themselves. 2) The ways in which they interact with one another. 3) The time they spend together. 4) The various pressures, expectations, and demands of others. Different groups have different personalities.

Types of Groups - The formal group is made up of individuals within the company who are out to achieve a set of specific goals. The

133

formal group operation can be studied, rearranged, and made to change. Of course making a formal group change does not mean that you will be successful. The problem occurs more often in informal groups because they easily form into cliques. If you belong to a clique and you are one of the insiders then you function along with the group. If you do not belong to the clique you may find problems in your employment, which is unfortunate since it makes for an unhappy employee and tends to reduce the level of morale within the group. The clique or informal group can change the operation of the formal group. There are many factors including group competition which can be either healthy or unhealthy for the organization. Coping with the clique, instead of fighting it, is important for the supervisor. The supervisor copes by accepting the clique as a fact of life, by asking for the cooperation of the informal leaders, by trying to prevent inner competition which causes battles, by avoiding forcing individuals to choose between the supervisor and a group, and by building a team spirit. (Morale will be discussed in Volume I, Lesson 8)

The individual is motivated when he or she can find happiness in the work situation. Management's role in meeting the needs involves the process of providing an appropriate environment. The individual also seeks personal and professional satisfaction by working with groups.

SUMMARY

An understanding of human needs and wants as well as the supervisor's role in satisfying them is important for an organization, Unrealized expectations lead to frustration and stress which may be harmful to the individual and organization.

LESSON DISCUSSION

I. WHY WE DO WHAT WE DO, AND WHEN WE DO IT

Our decisions are based on the sum of all our wants, desires, needs, and fears.

EXAMPLE: Each morning when the alarm rings our minds go through the process of deciding whether or not to go to work.

IN FAVOR OF
STAYING HOME

1. I was up late last night and I am very sleepy.

2. My garden or house needs attention.

3. There is a good ball game today.

4. It looks like rain, and if I get wet I will end up in the hospital.

5. It is Friday! It is the end of the week anyhow.

IN FAVOR OF
GOING TO WORK

1. I need the money for so many things.

2. I know that absenteeism is evaluated for promotions.

3. The last time I went to the ball game, the administrator saw me there.

4. I must get those reports out.

5. Today is payday.

RESULT: I get up and go to work!

135

The action we initiate is a result of the previous approach.

1. A basic law of human nature is that most voluntary action is based on the desire of each person for certain tangible or intangible possessions that will bring the person happiness.

2. The voluntary action is based on three factors:

    a. The person must feel a want for something.
    b. The person must believe or hope that his/her action will satisfy the want.
    c. The person must retain this belief long enough for the action to take place.

Five of the most important things that people want.

1. To feel more important, more worthy, and more worthwhile.

    a. Self-respect
    b. Self-esteem
    c. EXAMPLE: Always "honestly" try to find something worthwhile in each employee. Praise him/her for it.
    d. EXAMPLE: When someone gives you credit, give the credit to your employees.

    e. Have an employees' lunch each year. Give out service awards for longevity, best attendance record, and outstanding service.
    f. EXAMPLE: Tell your employee this is an important but difficult job. It is going to take a lot of effort to make the project succeed.
    g. Remember - EGO is greater than PROFIT.
    h. Send each employee a birthday card on his/her birthday.

2. To live safely, securely, and comfortably (Self-preservation).
    a. Self-preservation is a basic drive. Use it in safety campaigns, or in teaching infection control.
    b. An individual has to feel assured that the job is permanent. An individual that performs well has to feel secure in earning a living in this job for many years.
    c. Personal comfort is achieved by means of breaks or changes in assignment to relieve monotony.

3. To find the right mate and rear a family.
    a. Mention the awards which are received by family

136

members in the organization's newspaper.
b. Family picnics.
c. Invite wives or husbands once a year for a lunch.
d. Make the job family oriented.
e. Ask the organization to present a scholarship to a needy child of an employee.

4. To explore the unknown; to satisfy curiosity.
   a. Let the employee know how the job relates to the organization.
   b. Simply describe new innovative techniques.

5. To occasionally escape serious reality, to be entertained, and to play.
   a. The personnel department should obtain reduced or free tickets for ball games. plays, and so on.
   b. Plan an all day chartered bus trip to a major city to see a major league baseball or football game. Take the family.

REMEMBER:

1. Your ideas and messages to the employees are only part of the messages each day.
2. Explain your ideas and messages with brief reasons if possible.

3. Reinforce your ideas:
   a. briefly in writing
   b. discuss them simply/briefly
   c. require the employee to know them
   d. demonstrate what you want
   e. let the employee practice and then show you
   f. mention the message periodically as a reminder

The part played by the emotions:
1. Interest, admiration, and respect create a fine job.
2. Disinterest, negativism, and fear create a miserable job.
3. All things are the same--the equipment, the materials, the procedures, the types of individuals. Only the emotions are different.
4. Glandular secretions are affected by the type of emotion. Therefore, actual physical signs can be an indicator of the emotions.

   a. EXAMPLE: Adrenaline

The imagination:
1. In our minds we can picture situations so realistically that we actually feel we have lived through them.
   a. EXAMPLE: Thurber's short story "The Secret Life of Walter Mitty," with Danny Kaye as Casper Milquetoast.

137

b. We may be living in poverty but we dream of the day we can travel extensively or live in a beautiful home.

2. Imagination leads to an emotional change which creates a want and leads to a physical change.

3. The combinations of reason and dreaming leads to change.

4. Daydreaming may lead to accidents.

The nervous system as the organ of learning.

1. Our nervous system is a vast array of electrical lines, with our brain serving as the switchboard.
   a. Established pathways-- stimulus excites a certain response.
   b. You always drive home by a certain route. Today you are supposed to turn off and go downtown to meet your spouse--you continue on home instead.

2. Establishing good habits through new connections--this is an example of a good hook-up.

The law of learning includes:

1. Intensity of experiences.
2. Frequency of experiences.
3. Recentness of experiences.

II. GOOD HUMAN RELATIONS

In order to develop good human relations it is necessary to understand that each individual acts, thinks, and feels differently than every other individual. It is also necessary to understand that the attitude which the individual possesses is part of the total mental state which influences him/her to do certain things. Although you may have varying groups of individuals with the same skills, they will perform at different levels based on their attitudes. These attitudes are determined by past experience, the current environment, and by the individual's desires for certain things. Where the organization has good morale the individual tends to also exhibit good morale because the employee is in a happy and well-adjusted environment.

It must be understood that both men and women work for a variety of reasons. In order to make these workers happy the supervisor and administrators must satisfy the following needs:

1. Financial gain. Obviously you work to earn money in order to pay for the things that you need and want. However, money is not the only need an individual has and if other needs are not satisfied the worker will become unhappy, do a poor job, and possibly become a problem.

2. Job security is needed in order to help the individual plan for the future and for the individual to have

138

a feeling of relaxation in his or her work.

3. The worker should have a clearly defined task. Where the job is ambiguous or full of constantly changing situations and demands, the individual cannot find happiness in his or her work.

4. Workers must belong to the overall group in the organization. It is this feeling of togetherness that makes a strong organization.

5. We all need and want recognition for a job well done. Recognition can be given by promotions, increases in pay, being praised in public, or through special awards.

6. Everyone needs to feel that the work he or she is doing is worthwhile and will lead to an accomplishment.

7. The self-respect of the individual is essential. Whatever the job may be, the individual must be able to have respect during and after the work is completed.

8. Working conditions - especially the provisions of a safe, clean, and pleasing environment - has a profound effect upon the work which is being done. Good lighting and good ventilation are essential parts of good working conditions.

9. There needs to be a constant flow of communications between the employees and the supervisors as well as between the administrators and the supervisors. This line of communications will tend to disrupt rumors and keep everyone informed of the fine operation of the organization.

**We All Need And Want
Recognition For a Job Well Done**

10. Employees work best when they have good leadership that sets the proper outer boundaries of control.

Creating the proper working conditions is an essential part of the supervisors work. It is up to the supervisor to recognize when the working conditions are becoming poorer and when changes need to be made.

Good human relations is not just common sense, because what is common sense for one supervisor is not necessarily common sense for another. The important thing to understand is made up of two important words. The word "human" really means the individuals who are within the situation. The word "relations" means the way in which the individuals get along in a variety of situations. Often supervisors say, "Why don't the employees act the way I want them to"? The answer is simple-- people are unpredictable. They may act rationally in some situations and irrationally in others. Action and reaction is not simply due to what is occurring at work but is influenced by their home problems, home environment, happiness and failures, desires, beliefs, and the way in which they react to other individuals.

The main object of good human relations is not to avoid argument, discussion, or appropriate information, but rather to be able to express your concerns, discontents, and anger in a positive manner in order to resolve the problems and continue with the work.

Remember that the success of the individual in his/her job is a result of his/her environment at work and at home; the individual's needs, desires, and the ability to perform well; and most importantly, the manner in which the supervisor recognizes the above items and can compensate for problems and motivate the individual to do a good job.

III. WORK GROUPS AND HUMAN RELATIONS

Group dynamics is the way in which individuals in a group interact with each other under a variety of situations. The good supervisor recognizes this interaction and is then able to make necessary corrections where the interaction is poor or reinforces where the interaction is good.

To utilize the group properly, the supervisor should discuss with the individuals the goals of the organization and ask them to give some ideas on how best to meet these goals. Where the group participates in goal setting they are most apt to participate vigorously in attempting to achieve these goals.

It is important to solicit from the individual the kind of information that is necessary in order to make the group work properly. This information will be forthcoming if the supervisors give necessary assistance in providing a good work atmosphere so that individuals can state their problems, concerns, and recommendations.

IV. THE ROLE OF TRUST AND CONFIDENCE

One of the most important factors in supervision is the trust and confidence an employee places in the supervisor. The supervisor is the person in charge and to the employee this person represents the organization. Therefore, what the supervisor says and how it is said is essential in making the employee happy and in helping the employee perform at a maximum level of efficiency. The supervisor must be ethical and fair in dealing with the employees. In order to achieve this, the supervisor must be mature, have good control of his/her emotions, be able to recognize some mistakes, and be self-confident but not cocky.

V. MOTIVATION

Motivation, for our purposes, may be defined as someone getting to do something you want them to do because they want to do it. Since no two people are alike, different techniques are needed to motivate different individuals. The successful coach, general, administrator or supervisor, all have the same thing in common: they are able to get the individuals to perform and be happy because they are performing. A key point of motivation is for you, the supervisor, to have a good attitude toward your job. A good subordinate closely monitors your attitude. When your attitude is good, the employee's attitude will tend to be good. An important part of motivation is in evaluating and praising the employees for the things they have accomplished. Always give credit to individuals who deserve credit. Motivation means involving people. People look at the problems and goals, and find ways of rearranging and improving upon the techniques to be used. They implement these techniques in such a way that they are able to get pride out of their work. Good motivation also involves

good communication. The topic of communications will be discussed in Management and Supervision, Volume II.

The following list includes the items which are necessary in order to provide positive motivation:

1. You should strive to create a work atmosphere that is open, friendly, and encourages the formation of new ideas.

2. Study each job and employee carefully and make sure that the employee is matched properly to the job.

3. Make sure that the employee is part of the work team.

4. Do not play favorites.

5. Encourage flexibility whenever possible.

6. Provide pleasant physical surroundings.

7. You yourself must be motivated at all times.

8. Make each individual feel important.

9. Help the individual to improve himself/herself.

10. Involve the individual as much as possible in the decision-making process.

VI. MOTIVATIONAL TECHNIQUES

Research has demonstrated that if the supervisor will follow the above- mentioned material and the techniques which follow, the employees will be more likely to be motivated in an effective manner.

1. Be supportive and friendly. Do not be hostile.

2. Understand the needs of the group. Do not allow peer pressure to interfere with the individual trying to improve.

3. Recognize that the employees are important and are human beings and must be treated as such.

4. Make sure you have a reasonable level of expectation.

5. Use training and development programs to help develop and build the individual.

6. Set goals for the group with their help and consultations.

7. Aid the individual in developing better technical confidence.

8. Provide effective leadership for the group.

9. Establish a set of mutually accepted objectives.

10. Recognize that in order to get an effective job done the supervisor must be liked, well respected, and always firm but fair in decision making.

VII. SUMMARY

The "Fundamental Management Information" Section discussed human needs and wants, the supervisor's and manager's role in satisfying these needs and wants, frustration and stress, motivation, formal and informal groups and how they influence the individual, and their role in motivation.

Obviously, many texts have been written concerning the understanding of human behavior. It is the function of this course to give some background in understanding human behavior, but more importantly to give a series of concrete recommendations on how best to work with the employees.

LESSON 6
CASE PROBLEM 1

The Hospital Disaster

Sally Harris, the administrator of the Potack Regional Hospital, was advised by Jill Snowcraft, the Nursing Director, that many of her employees were upset by recent administrative decisions. An efficiency team had surveyed the hospital and made several recommendations on how to get more work out of the staff. They recommended that the staff be assigned to all shifts at random to alleviate extra personnel on certain shifts and too few personnel on other shifts. They stated that 20% of the staff should float to all areas; after all, if they are RNs they should be able to do everything. They recommended that all supervisors and patient care managers be immediately reviewed and reduced to staff positions, if needed. In the future all supervisory staff should be reviewed for possible demotion once a year, if they did not meet the stated objectives. All new orientation would be reduced from six weeks to one week. All overtime would be canceled, since overtime was an indication of poor management.

1. What error did Sally Harris make in accepting and implementing the report of the efficiency team?

2. What error did Jill Snowcraft make in not discussing with Sally Harris the implications of such administrative decisions on the nursing department, before the decisions were turned into hospital policy?

3. What needs do working people have that are being violated by the new policies?

4. How would you handle this situation?

ANSWER SHEET

LESSON 6
CASE PROBLEM 1

MANAGEMENT AND SUPERVISION FOR WORKING PROFESSIONALS

LESSON 6
CASE PROBLEM 2

POLITICS - What a Way to Run an Agency

Dr. Leu Powers, the director of the state EPA, was appointed by Governor Carwell to make appropriate changes in the troubled agency. Dr. Powers had been an excellent fund-raiser and of course had administrative training. Dr. Powers called together all department heads and asked them to submit a report in two weeks on how to improve the agency. The reports indicated that many people had been hired haphazardly, did not necessarily meet job specifications, assignments were rigidly set forth, individuals worked independently and were not part of an overall team, goals and objectives were unrealistic, and the ventilation and lighting in the building were poor. Dr. Powers response to the reports was to mandate a change in all areas in 90 days to meet new policies, goals, and objectives. Anyone not complying would be fired and replaced by someone from the proper party.

1. Why were there problems existing at the State EPA?

2. What is your reaction to enforcing new policies, goals, and objectives in 90 days, or fire the individuals who are not complying?

3. What do you think about replacing employees with people from the "right" party?

4. What innovative techniques would you use to improve the work produced?

5. What do you think of the work environment and its effect on people?

ANSWER SHEET

LESSON 6
CASE PROBLEM 2

MANAGEMENT AND SUPERVISION FOR WORKING PROFESSIONALS

PRACTICAL EXERCISES

You may do any two or more of these items.

1. Determine if you are satisfying each of the ten major needs of your workers as listed in the study guide. If you are not, determine why not and how you can do this in a practical manner so that the individual will be a better employee.

2. Evaluate the work of your employees and determine if they are being positively motivated in a proper manner. Use the list of items within the Lesson Discussion notes as a guide.

3. Make a checklist of the motivational techniques listed and determine if you are following these techniques with your workers. If not, determine how you can improve upon this area.

4. Determine if wages are the overriding concern of your group. If not, determine what the overriding concerns are and how you can attempt to satisfy them.

LESSON 6
PRACTICAL EXERCISES ANSWER SHEET

MANAGEMENT AND SUPERVISION FOR WORKING PROFESSIONALS

Do two exercises and number them. Use additional paper if necessary.

SELF-TESTING EXAMINATION #6

TRUE-FALSE QUESTIONS (CORRECT ANSWERS APPEAR ON PAGE 150)

1. Supervisors and managers must always be aware of human needs to be successful.   1. __

2. All individuals experience frustration on the job.   2. __

3. Stress is always harmful.   3. __

4. It is not necessary for individuals to participate in decision making.   4. __

5. Motivation is always positive for all employees since they are being paid.   5. __

6. Group competition is always good.   6. __

7. Financial gain is the most important reason why people work.   7. __

8. Creating the proper working conditions is an essential part of the work of a supervisor.   8. __

9. The main objective of good human relations is not to avoid discussion or discontent, but rather to express concerns and discontents in a positive manner which will clear them up and then continue with the work.   9. __

10. The results of an individual's work is based on his/her work environment, home environment, wants, needs, desires, ability to perform, and least importantly the ability of the supervisor to carry out the job.   10. __

11. In this modern era of the Equal Rights Amendment, females must be treated the same as males and not be given any special consideration at any time.   11. __

12. One of the key motivators in the organization is the first line supervisor.   12. __

13. The good supervisor helps motivate employees by providing an open, friendly, and pleasant work environment.   13. __

149

ANSWERS TO LESSON 6 SELF-TESTING EXAMINATION

If your answer is incorrect, go back to the material referred to and determine why your answer is incorrect.

QUESTIONS FROM FUNDAMENTAL MANAGEMENT INFORMATION SECTION

1. T Beginning of Fundamental Management Information
2. T Beginning of Fundamental Management Information
3. F Middle of Fundamental Management Information
4. F Middle of Fundamental Management Information
5. F End of Fundamental Management Information
6. F End of Fundamental Management Information

QUESTIONS FROM LESSON DISCUSSION

7. F Middle of Lesson Discussion
8. T Middle of Lesson Discussion
9. T Middle of Lesson Discussion
10. F Middle of Lesson Discussion
11. F End of Lesson Discussion
12. T End of Lesson Discussion
13. T End of Lesson Discussion

CASE PROBLEM 1 ANSWERS

The Hospital Disaster

1. Sally should have met with the Nursing Director and discussed the report before making any decisions. The Nursing Director would have explained the implications of such actions.

2. Apparently, Jill was not involved with the consulting team. The administrator and consultants made the decisions independently. If she was aware of the recommendations but did not speak up to defend her nurses, then she was a poor director. She should have explained to Sally the problems these new policies would cause among the nurses.

3. The work shift is of utmost importance to people. Coordination with a spouse's schedule, being with children at a certain time of the day or night, or other personal obligations determine what work shift is best for each person. It would be almost impossible to find sitters for a shift that constantly changes. Changing shifts may lead to illness and absenteeism because the person would have problems trying to adjust to sleeping at different times of day. Employees perform better when they work in an environment where they are relaxed and comfortable. People feel very insecure and unsure when moved to strange working assignments. Efficiency and competency are lowered when nurses are removed from areas of expertise. Supervisors lose their sense of security when they discover they can be demoted immediately (or in the future) if they do not meet certain requirements. Orientation is needed to acquaint new employees with rules, regulations, and procedures of the new job and to train them to carry it out in an appropriate manner. Overtime pay is not always an indication of poor management. It often indicates a loyal and caring employee who stays with a patient until a crisis is past or one who does not walk out and leave a grieving family.

4. Do not immediately implement the recommendations made by the efficiency team because they obviously do not have hospital experience. This consulting firm should have been thoroughly investigated before hiring to determine if they understood the hospital environment and quality control. Since the error was already made, a memo should be sent to employees informing them that all new procedures would be curtailed until the situation could be studied further. Ask for their patience during this transitional period while an attempt is made to find the best way to improve hospital efficiency. Discuss the recommendations with the Director of Nursing before implementing any rules. Have the Director of Nursing work with her staff and supervisors to find better ways to deal with the problems identified by the consulting team.

CASE PROBLEM 2 ANSWERS

POLITICS - What a Way to Run an Agency

1. Problems existed at the state EPA because of past hiring practices; positions were filled with unqualified individuals; there was no flexibility in assignments; there was a lack of a team concept; there was an unrealistic set of goals and objectives; and poor working conditions existed.

2. The enforcement of new policies, goals, and objectives in a 90-day period was unrealistic and only led to new problems. Threatening people with firing is counter- productive. It causes resentment and anger.

3. Politics should not be part of hiring practices in a professional, or in fact any type of work situation. It does not address the issue of hiring unqualified individuals.

4. The quality and quantity of work can be improved by establishing realistic goals and objectives and developing an interdisciplinary team to work on assignments. Address issues of unqualified personnel who are assigned work they are incapable of completing.

5. The work environment has a profound effect on the people working there. It has a direct impact on the quality and quantity of work.

LESSON 7

FIRM, BUT FAIR - HOW TO DEAL WITH PEOPLE

LEARNING OBJECTIVES

When you have successfully completed this lesson, you should:

1. Understand that the supervisor must be firm in actions and approaches to the employees but at the same time the supervisor must be fair.

2. Understand the human problem of control and how to make human control more effective.

3. Recognize that a good supervisor has authority but utilizes this authority wherever possible in a pleasant manner.

4. Recognize the nature of authority, and the types of supervision which are used.

5. Understand the art of leadership and some of the techniques used in leadership.

6. Understand how to win employee cooperation.

7. Recognize that leadership must involve developing trust and confidence in the individual and that the supervisor must use wisdom and empathy.

FUNDAMENTAL MANAGEMENT INFORMATION

INTRODUCTION

Management must exercise appropriate authority while encouraging good human relations.

Authority is the right to command or give orders. The way an individual is able to influence others is called power. Supervisors and managers have both authority and power, however it is the positive use of it which aids in control of programs and people to achieve appropriate objectives.

The goal of good human relations includes the following: (1) Know and understand each person as an individual. (2) Approach and supervise each person as an individual. (3) Help the individual achieve satisfaction out of that which he or she is doing. (4) Get each individual to contribute to the total effort. (5) Foster cooperation between and among subordinates, peers, administrators, and supervisors.

SUPERVISOR'S AND MANAGER'S ROLE

The supervisor exercises authority and encourages good human relations. In this human relations role the supervisor or manager act as an educator, counselor, and judge and also relates information accurately to subordinates. Each of these roles is discussed later in greater detail in

several different lessons. The supervisor or manager as a judge includes the sub-roles of evaluator, enforcer, arbitrator, and the dispenser of proper justice as needed. The emphasis of good human relations essentially is the use of positive approaches to the function of supervision and management related to control.

CONTROL

Control is making something happen the way it was planned to happen. Control is the process of taking the necessary actions to insure that the objectives of the organization are accomplished in an effective and efficient manner. Control should be positive whenever possible. Control is a normal, pervasive and positive force. It is only effective when it guides someone's behavior. Successful control is related to future success. It is a dynamic approach. Control relates to all sorts of human endeavors. Controlling is the process managers go through to control. The controlling system consists of measuring performance, comparing measured performance to standards, and taking corrective action. Before managers can determine what is effective and efficient they must be able to establish standards related to what they want to accomplish. These standards should be performance related. They may consist of certain levels of quantity and quality which can be measured. Control can start during the training process when the individual is taught the proper way to do things. It continues happening and continues further when the individuals give feedback to the supervisor and the supervisor gives feedback to the individuals concerning their performance.

Barriers - There are several potential barriers to successful control. They include: (1) An undesirable emphasis on driving people to produce huge quantities of work on a short-term basis without thinking of long-term results. (2) Control activities which can increase employee frustration and reduce morale. (3) Control activities which can result in falsification of reports and records since the employee is trying to keep pace with that which is being demanded. (4) Control activities which can limit the individuals' ability to think in a positive and constructive manner and thereby causes the individual, the group, and the organization to have a very narrow perspective. (5) Control activities which may become an end in themselves rather than a means of obtaining objectives which have been established.

Symptoms - Symptoms of inadequate control include: (1) An unexplained decline in quantity or quality of work. (2) An increase in consumer complaints. (3) Employee dissatisfaction shown by complaints, grievances, and substantial personnel turnover. (4) Personnel not performing. (5) A disorganized operation with excessive paper work.

SUMMARY

The use of appropriate systems of authority in a constructive manner which recognizes the need for good human relations creates a positive environment where employees will be motivated to meet the goals and objectives of the organization.

LESSON DISCUSSION

I. THE NATURE OF CONTROL

Control is the final function of the supervisor. In order for the supervisor to get the work completed, he/she first plans the work, then organizes it, and finally exercises the necessary control to get the work done. It is a function in which the supervisor directs others, guides, teaches, issues orders and directives, and encourages individuals to work at a high level of proficiency. When control is exercised in a negative manner, the individual may rebel. Because of control, standards are set up that can be used to measure the performance of the individual employee. The standards established should be reasonable, achievable, and whenever possible should take into consideration the needs of the employees.

II. THE HUMAN PROBLEM OF CONTROL

Since people are not machines and each person differs individually, the techniques used to exercise proper control must be modified to meet the situation and the individual. Problems occur because people generally do not like to be controlled. If the individuals realize that the following conditions exist, then they may well rebel or slow down their work. These conditions are

1. Improper standards

2. Improperly administered standards

3. The amount of production required always seems to increase

4. Inaccurate measurements of success

5. Use of poor corrective measures such as personal criticism

6. An inability to understand the reason for the controls

People Are Not Machines

As a result of improper controls, individuals may become highly resistant and, therefore, refuse to carry out their work. Resistance may occur not only in the individuals but in the group or through open

157

conflict between various levels of staff within the organization.

III. MAKING HUMAN CONTROL MORE EFFECTIVE

The trained, competent supervisor is keenly aware of human aspects of control. The supervisor not only adapts the control techniques to the individual job, but also shows that he or she is part of the working force by not being afraid to do anything anybody else does, getting dirty at work right along with the employees, and assisting when a crisis arises and helping resolve the problems. The smart supervisor also looks at some of the personal problems that the individual has and attempts to give assistance in this area. Personal problems, home environment, working environment, and the needs of the individual are very much interrelated.

Supervisors should realize that some errors are made accidentally. These errors should be handled in a very gentle manner. The individual should not be reprimanded for these errors but should be instructed in correcting the situation and preventing errors from occurring again. If the situation continues, the supervisor needs to sit down with the worker and discuss and search for the underlying causes of the problem. Is there an emotional problem? Is the individual having some physical stress? Is the individual sick? These are the basic questions that the supervisor must determine as he/she attempts to affect the

control over the employee. Remember the goal of control is to get better achievement, not irritate, harass, or build up the stature of the supervisor.

IV. THE FIRST MEETING WITH THE NEW EMPLOYEE

During the initial meeting with the new employee all of the necessary company policies and procedures should be openly discussed. What is to be expected of both the employee and the supervisor should be clearly spelled out. This will create mutual understanding and enable both parties to begin work on an equal and pleasant basis.

V. A GOOD SUPERVISOR TRIES TO PLEASE

A good supervisor is always considerate of other individual's feelings. The more the supervisor considers the employees, the more considerate the employees will be in return.

The Good Supervisor Does Not Have To Assume The Stance Of A Chest-Pounding Supervisor

VI. THE NATURE OF AUTHORITY

When real authority is exercised, it does not have to be stated - the employees simply assume that the supervisor is in charge. The chest - pounding supervisor looks and acts like a gorilla, not like a fellow human being anxious to help the worker.

VII. TYPES OF SUPERVISION

The democratic supervisor is not only well liked but also receives the greatest cooperation from the largest number of employees.

The topics under Sections IV, V, VI, and VII are more fully discussed elsewhere in the Lesson and Fundamental Management Information.

VIII. THE ART OF LEADERSHIP

Leadership is the ability to get other people to follow you and willingly do what you ask of them. The very best leaders are able to win friends and to gain respect from people around them. This does not mean that the supervisor has to be "buddy-buddy" with his/her workers. After all, a parent would like to be a friend to his/her children but still must be the leader. A good leader instinctively knows where and when to be somewhat removed from a situation. Likewise, the leader also realizes when to

be a full member in the friendship circle of the employees. Being a good leader is a hard job. However, the rewards are plentiful. A good leader means having prestige and status among others. The supervisor is able to clearly see what his/her accomplishments are, and is able to take considerable pride in the work which has been completed.

Although some individuals have natural leadership qualities, most of us need to be trained in the specific goals of leadership. The leader must know the following:

1. The leader should know in what direction he/she is headed and have confidence in his/her own ability to lead others in the proper direction.

2. The leader must be willing to give up certain rights in order to accomplish the job.

3. The supervisor must be an individual of high character. This person should not be afraid to admit mistakes and must be able to accept criticism.

4. A good leader is a competent individual.

5. The leader must have good judgment and be able to utilize judgment in a tactful and wise manner.

6. The leader must exhibit the proper way of doing things. Perhaps this means coming to work ahead of time and not leaving until the work is finished. The leader is eager to carry

out the tasks which have been assigned. Does this mean that a good leader cannot have a down day? Of course not. As is true with any other individual, a good leader will have both exhilarating and frustrating days. The difference, however, is that the supervisor must limit the verbal and non verbal signals attached to frustrations and attempt to make the work environment a happy one for all.

A good leader is predictable and has the ability to put himself/herself into the employee's shoes. The leader is concerned with employees' welfare, treats employees in an equal manner, and constantly shows enthusiasm. To complete a job in a satisfactory manner, a good leader will carry out the following steps:

- Gather the necessary information to solve the problems.

- Assemble and assimilate the information in a logical manner.

- Plan the group goals and objectives.

- Help determine the necessary course of action.

- Get the right person for the right job.

- Issue clear and simple instructions.

- Keep the employees informed of what is going on.

- Lead and motivate employees.

- Give additional suggestions, instructions, and information as needed to help accomplish the tasks.

- Evaluate the results in a fair manner.

- Always seek advice from the employees in order to try to improve the techniques utilized.

IX. WINNING EMPLOYEE COOPERATION

Not all employees will cooperate with the supervisor. It is recognized that money alone will not get the employee to cooperate and do a necessary job. The employee seeks not only salary but also the opportunity to meet with other individuals and be part of the group. The employee needs to be able to gain self-satisfaction and recognition from his/her work. The best way to win employee cooperation is to be straightforward, simple in your approach, friendly, and helpful. Stop giving orders--listen to what the individuals have to say. There may be problems you are not aware of. If you listen and resolve them, you will win the employee's cooperation. Later on in this course, there will be further discussion about how to handle specific types of employee problems and how to handle the problem employee. No matter how hard the supervisor may try, the problem itself may be within the employee and one which can only be resolved through necessary disciplinary action. This area will be discussed later.

X. HOW TO GIVE INSTRUCTIONS

When you give instructions or issue orders, be confident but not cocky; be calm, firm and pleasant but not irritable and demanding. Always attempt to select the right person for the right job. Instructions should be given as a request rather than a command. Most people will object when they are ordered to do things. On the other hand, they will be happy to assist you when they are requested to do so.

If an employee refuses to carry out the request, do not get angry and start to berate him/her by threatening to fire the individual. Find out why the person objects. Possibly the order is not an intelligent decision or perhaps the order, if carried out, will cause extreme danger. There may be other reasons why the order should not be carried out. After you have discussed this with the individual and if there is still no response, then it is necessary to consider further types of action. It is most important to note that the technique of requesting may not be applicable in emergency situations. When an emergency situation has occurred, it may be necessary to issue rapid but clear and simple orders which must be carried out in order to avoid danger to individuals or property.

If the individual is following your orders but not carrying them out in a proper manner, then it is necessary to determine if the person understands the order, if the employee has been trained properly, or if there are other extenuating circumstances. After you have made this determination, make the necessary corrections. Then, after the corrections have been made, if the individual still cannot carry out the orders properly it may be necessary to make a judgment as to whether to shift the individual to a new job or to take some form of disciplinary action. Never give an order when angry. Never use an impatient tone. Always assume that the problem in carrying out an order, at least initially, is due to circumstances other than the employee's unwillingness to carry out the order.

Avoid making the following errors in giving orders:

1. Do not give an order in an off-hand manner.

2. Do not assume the employee understands the order.

3. Do not give too many orders.

4. Do not give conflicting instructions.

5. Choose the willing employee when possible.

6. Do not pick on any one person habitually.

7. Do not give too much detail.

8. Do not be the gorilla pounding on his/her chest; act like a human being.

XI. LEADERSHIP STYLES AND PRACTICES

Leadership cannot be simply defined as one of several techniques you utilize in given situations to achieve specific goals. Leadership is the technique of motivating individuals in a friendly and happy way to do what you would like them to do. Unfortunately, some people consider leadership to be the use of force. Force is the supervisor's ability to fire, reprimand, reduce salary, or belittle an employee. None of these techniques is good. Enticement is a technique in which the individual is promised a variety of rewards for achieving certain goals. This may be overtime pay, promotion, or even a trip to Hawaii. Enticement can be used on a limited basis. However, remember that an individual must get a certain amount of good "inner feeling" from the job. Money and rewards are not enough to create a happy employee.

Manipulation is a technique utilized to get people to do things - not because they necessarily want to, but because they feel they are compelled to. One good example of manipulation is the child who constantly cries. The mother, therefore, feeds or holds the child in order to take care of the needs of the child. Unfortunately, much of the crying is a good attention-getter; the child has manipulated the mother into doing things she really did not want to do.

Intrinsic motivation is perhaps one of the most pleasant techniques used in leadership. In this technique, the individual employee is able to identify himself or herself with the company and the supervisors. The employee builds his/her ego because he/she is intensely involved. The employees take pride in their work because they have accomplished something very worthwhile. They go to work in the morning challenged and happy to face a new day; they leave at the end of the day knowing the satisfaction of having contributed fully towards their own welfare and the welfare of the organization.

Unfortunately, in our society we are losing much of the intrinsic value of work. Many people are being paid all too well for doing too little work.

XII. TRUST AND CONFIDENCE

Proper placement of trust and confidence are major factors in achieving the goals of the organization. The employees must have trust and confidence in their supervisors and faith that the organization will carry out its part of the bargain. The employees should always feel that when they have been told something it is true, necessary, and accurate. Since it is impossible and undesirable to write down every part and bit of every agreement reached between people, the people must have trust in each other. If, for example, a supervisor says to an employee, "If we can meet this emergency order and still keep our regular work going properly, I will make sure that you get compensatory time or additional wages" it is necessary for the supervisor to live up to the promises made. The only way to achieve true trust and confidence is for the individuals, especially the supervisor, to be mature, have self-confidence, and possess a certain degree of humility.

XIII. WISDOM AND EMPATHY

A supervisor must be knowledgeable about the work environment and must show empathy for the employees. The supervisor must understand the uniqueness of each individual, give recognition to the individual, and also realize that the individual seeks satisfaction in all parts of his/her living relationships with other people. It is necessary for the supervisor to have self-esteem and self-respect and not only instill this in the employees, but also emphasize that he/she respects the work of the employees and is willing to help and guide them to attain higher goals.

Empathy is extremely important in situations where the employees are having problems. The supervisor should recognize these problems and attempt to assist the individual in developing some good solutions.

XIV. SUMMARY

The "Fundamental Management Information" section discussed the goal of human relations, control, barriers to control, and symptoms of inadequate control.

Throughout this lesson the major emphasis has been on being fair and firm with the employees. It is essential that the

supervisor acts as a reasonable person and guides employees to reach the goals of the organization as well as their own goals. The good supervisor must keep the unit working in a satisfactory manner. But the good supervisor must constantly recognize that he/she is dealing with people and must strive to be a person who respects and assists other human beings. A supervisor needs to think, "Would I like to be treated in the way in which I am treating my employees?"

163

LESSON 7
CASE PROBLEM 1

Firm and Unfair

John Winters, the Environmental Health Director, had taken numerous courses in administration and supervision. What impressed him most was his thought that control over people was the best approach to get the results to help him reach higher positions. He planned and organized all work without consulting supervisors and technical personnel. When Jodi Stevens objected to being constantly ordered around, he disciplined her. He established unrealistic standards of performance without input from others and administered them at whim. He demanded more and more work from the staff and provided less and less assistance. Tim Farrow was loudly criticized in front of his colleagues for failure to meet the new standards of the quantity of work being demanded. John Winters was really going to show everyone how to get a job done. Angry employees created public relations problems when they carried out their assignments The commissioners were deluged by complaints from the public about the employees.

1. What should have John Winters learned from his courses?

2. Was it the university's fault that problems were occurring in the Environmental Health Department?

3. What did John Winters do wrong in dealing with Jodi Stevens and Tim Farrow?

4. What other errors did he make in controlling people?

5. How would you rectify this situation?

ANSWER SHEET

**LESSON 7
CASE PROBLEM 1**

MANAGEMENT AND SUPERVISION FOR WORKING PROFESSIONALS

LESSON 7
CASE PROBLEM 2

Leadership - The George Stillwell Way

Dr. George Stillwell was a brilliant scientist and as a result was chosen to be the administrator of the Jackson-Duval City County Health Department. He elected to take the job and to leave State University because he had a young family and the additional $30,000 a year would be helpful. Unfortunately, his administrative experience was limited to having been a department chairperson. After 6 months he still did not have a clear understanding of the direction he wanted the department to take and therefore often gave conflicting instructions to his division directors. His uncertainty caused him to hold on to all authority, thereby making his office the only place where decisions could be made. He was very sensitive to all criticism and would not accept suggestions. Although highly competent and a recognized author and speaker in his own area, he knew little or nothing about many of the components of the department. When problems arose he either hid from the situation or was very tactless in dealing with his subordinates. His instructions were complex and usually based on limited knowledge of the situation.

1. What mistake did the board make in hiring Dr. Stillwell?

2. Was his decision to take the job a wise one, knowing that his knowledge of many programs was limited or nonexistent?

3. Did he understand the art of leadership?

4. What could he do to improve his leadership skills?

ANSWER SHEET

LESSON 7
CASE PROBLEM 2

MANAGEMENT AND SUPERVISION FOR WORKING PROFESSIONALS

PRACTICAL EXERCISES

You may do any two or more of these items.

1. Make a list of all the items which are important when you meet with a new employee. Then, determine if you are following each of these items.

2. Determine if you are a helpful supervisor and if you are getting your workers to perform properly as a result of the supervisory techniques which you are using.

3. Determine how to exercise your authority. Are you a chest-pounder or do you urge others to work with you and get them to perform their job in a satisfactory manner because they want to?

4. Utilizing the list of specific goals of leadership found in the Lesson Discussion material determine if you are meeting each of these goals and if you are not, why not?

5. Do you follow leadership roles by carrying out the steps set forth in the Lesson Discussion? The eleven steps should help you determine whether or not you are thinking of the employee as a part of your role of being a good leader.

6. How do you go about getting cooperation from employees? Write down your answers and determine if they are really satisfactory.

7. When you give instructions, are your instructions clear, to the point, and presented in a proper manner? Evaluate yourself. Determine if you are making the unnecessary errors of instruction giving which are found in the Lesson Discussion.

8. Determine how you act as a leader. Do you use force, enticement, manipulation, motivation? How successful are you in this role?

9. Determine if the employees have trust and confidence in you by writing down the number of times they come to you to seek some sort of assistance with either on-the-job or off-the-job problems.

LESSON 7
PRACTICAL EXERCISES ANSWER SHEET

MANAGEMENT AND SUPERVISION FOR WORKING PROFESSIONALS

Do two exercises and number them. Use additional paper if necessary.

SELF-TESTING EXAMINATION #7

TRUE-FALSE QUESTIONS (CORRECT ANSWERS APPEAR ON PAGE 172)

1. The goal of good human relations is to foster an excellent work environment.　　1. __

2. The supervisor or manager is an educator, counselor, and judge.　　2. __

3. Control is a necessary but negative technique.　　3. __

4. Control is a function of supervision. It means to direct others, guide others, teach others, or encourage others to carry out their work.　　4. __

5. In order to make human control more effective a supervisor must show that he/she is part of the working force.　　5. __

6. Supervisors must understand that errors cannot be tolerated and, therefore, necessary reprimands should be issued.　　6. __

7. A good supervisor is a considerate individual. The more considerate he/she is of the employees the weaker they believe the supervisor to be.　　7. __

8. When you have real authority and you use it, it is important for you to state that you have the authority so other people will understand it.　　8. __

9. A good leader always gathers necessary information before solving a problem.　　9. __

10. A good leader issues clear necessary information before solving a problem.　　10. __

11. When you give instructions, always be confident, calm, firm, and pleasant. However, at times this philosophy is set aside and you must be demanding in order to get the job done.　　11. __

12. If any employee begins to carry out a request and then refuses to go any further, a good technique to use is to threaten the individual.　　12. __

13. If an individual is following orders but not carrying them out in a proper manner, it is necessary to start the disciplinary process to make sure that the orders are carried out.　　13. __

14. A good supervisor does not give too many orders at one time.   14. __

15. A good supervisor does not give conflicting instructions.   15. __

16. Too many people are being paid too many dollars for doing too little work in our society today.   16. __

ANSWERS TO LESSON 7 SELF-TESTING EXAMINATION

If your answer is incorrect, go back to the material referred to and determine why your answer is incorrect.

QUESTIONS FROM FUNDAMENTAL MANAGEMENT SECTION

1. T Beginning of Fundamental Management Information
2. T Beginning of Fundamental Management Information
3. F Middle of Fundamental Management Information

QUESTION FROM LESSON DISCUSSION

4. T Beginning of Lesson Discussion
5. T Beginning of Lesson Discussion
6. F Beginning of Lesson Discussion
7. F Beginning of Lesson Discussion
8. F Middle of Lesson Discussion
9. T Middle of Lesson Discussion
10. T Middle of Lesson Discussion
11. F End of Lesson Discussion
12. F End of Lesson Discussion
13. F End of Lesson Discussion
14. T End of Lesson Discussion
15. T End of Lesson Discussion
16. T End of Lesson Discussion

CASE PROBLEM 1 ANSWERS

Firm and Unfair

1. John Winters should have learned that the autocratic leadership style is least desirable and that power and control over people do not bring success. He should have worked in harmony with them and respected them. He should have learned to motivate subordinates to do the job, to be consistent, and not to expect the impossible.

2. No! Mr Winters learned the theory and art of management but applied them in an inappropriate manner.

3. He ordered Jodi to do work and then disciplined her for objecting. Her assignment should have been based on her qualifications and job description plus appropriate goals and objectives. Tim Farrow was given unrealistic standards for quantity of work. No consideration was given for fairness. Tim was publicly criticized. A good director does not have to constantly be on the employees if they are properly trained and well motivated.

4. He did all the planning and organizing on his own without consulting his staff. He was inconsistent. He did not enforce his own rules all of the time. He set unrealistic standards. His impossible demands and erratic behavior frustrated and upset the employees. Their anger showed in their work. He did not provide assistance to his employees. He showed everyone how to get the job done, without allowing them to participate in the decision-making process.

5. Set forth the appropriate way to manage a department. If changes do not occur in sixty days, consider moving John Winters to a position that does not require him to perform as a supervisor or department director.

CASE PROBLEM 2 ANSWERS

Leadership - The George Stillwell Way

1. The board hired an individual with relatively no managerial experience. The decision was based solely on his reputation and achievements.

2. It was not a wise decision. He was only financially motivated.

3. No, this is an example of a highly successful technical person without management skills put into a management position based on the premise that he will be a good manager, since he was successful as a scientist.

4. Dr. Stillwell could improve by learning the components of his department: networking with other division directors; developing a plan of action along with his supervisors and managers; making instructions clear, concise and consistent; delegating authority but maintaining ultimate responsibility for the programs; being open to constructive criticism and/or suggestions; addressing problems as they arise; and enrolling in a management course.

LESSON 8

MORALE

LEARNING OBJECTIVES

When you have successfully completed this lesson, you should:

1. Understand the meaning of morale, the factors influencing morale, and how to develop good morale.

2. Have learned how to measure and improve morale.

3. Understand the concepts of attitudes and morale.

4. Have learned practical elements of morale building.

FUNDAMENTAL MANAGEMENT INFORMATION

INTRODUCTION

An attitude is a state of mind that indicates certain opinions or beliefs about certain concepts. An opinion is a judgment and it generally reflects an attitude or outlook on life. An opinion is a verbal means of stating your attitude. Attitudes are developed over long periods of time as a result of the many cultural forces that shape personality. A good attitude is one that appears to conform with what the individual and possibly the supervisor wants. A bad attitude is one that does not conform to what the individual, and probably his/her supervisor wants. An important concept to understand is that an attitude might be good for one person while it is bad for someone else and vice versa. Therefore, you must have an understanding of the principles behind the attitude. The supervisor's attitude toward whatever is going on is extremely important since it influences subordinates. Your approach to things not only influences what you do but also influences the reactions of other.

SUPERVISOR'S BEHAVIOR

Supervisors need to understand how they influence their subordinates since their behavior may be the problem rather than the subordinates' behavior. Some of the problems that lead to poor responses by subordinates to their supervisors include: (1) Using threats. (2) Keeping people insecure. (3) Being unpredictable. (4) Being immature. (5) Not keeping promises. (6) Issuing conflicting orders and instructions. (7) Taking the glory for yourself when something is good and criticizing the individual when something is bad. (8) Disciplining people in front of others. (9) Holding grudges. (10) Playing favorites. 11) Establishing unrealistic standards. (12) Not enforcing standards in a uniform manner. (13) Not training subordinates to meet new situations.

IMPROVING EMPLOYEE BEHAVIOR

In order to change attitudes of individuals it is important to: (1) Identify the improper attitude or behavior. (2) Determine what supports this attitude or behavior. (3) Find techniques to weaken these supports. (4) Offer a substitute for the improper attitude or behavior. Good communications, proper persuasion, adequate participation and job enrichment help change attitudes which affect behavior. When the supervisor uses a positive means of attitude adjustment it is far more appropriate than using a negative technique for attitude adjustment. When subordinates are constantly criticized and subjected to hostility, ridicule, or intolerance, the subordinates suffer. When subordinates receive encouragement, praise, fairness, a sense of security, approval and acceptance, they thrive.

GOOD MORALE

Job satisfaction and supervisory and management enthusiasm contribute to good morale. Job satisfaction can be determined by use of surveys, levels of absenteeism, tardiness, job turnover, grievances and complaints. Job satisfaction occurs when individuals have self-esteem, and have positive expectations about their jobs. They understand the limitations, and have a good personal working relationship with others in the job situation.

CHANGE - A MORALE PROBLEM

Change can be the cause of poor morale since people typically fear change and may resist it. Change may necessitate the elimination of old jobs and the development of new jobs or certainly new specifications for the job. When individuals are faced with the unknown they may become unhappy, uncertain, or stressed and their morale drops accordingly. They feel that they have lost control. In order to avoid these kinds of problems subordinates should participate in the change and in the discussions leading up to the change. All participation should be done in a clear and concise manner. Individuals should understand what the change will do, how it will affect the organization, how the individual will benefit from the change and the potential problems related to the change. The problems may include an alteration of job style, having to learn new things, having to develop into a different type of

professional. Change can be extremely scary or can be a challenge, depending on how it is presented to the group.

QUALITY OF WORK LIFE

The quality of work life is extremely important for good morale. Quality of work life revolves around the work, the group, the organization, the individual, the supervisor, or manager, and the satisfaction that all feel when a proper job is carried out.

SUMMARY

Good morale is based on proper employee and supervisor attitudes. Attitudes can be adjusted by reinforcement of positive actions. Change can cause a morale problem or can lead to a new challenge and a better quality of work life.

LESSON DISCUSSION

I. THE MEANING OF MORALE

Morale is that special element that turns an average basketball team into a superior basketball team. It is that special feeling that keeps people working in a situation that appears to be hopeless, yet because of their great group effort they ultimately might succeed. Morale is the spirit and confidence with which workers carry out their jobs. Morale is that magnificent inner feeling of excitement and happiness when individuals work together. Poor morale is the opposite of all of this and results in absenteeism, dissension, anger, anguish, a lack of good feeling, hopelessness, and eventually poor performance.

II. FACTORS INFLUENCING MORALE

Rumors which are spread by individuals or groups cause fear, stress, or disagreement in the group or within the organization. Uncertainty, frustration, errors, and delays also influence morale. Supervisors and their attitudes constitute an important part of either good or poor morale. A supervisor with a good attitude promotes better morale in his/her workers. Morale may also be affected by wages, recognition, the amount of work accomplished, nature of the work, work conditions, and job security. The individual's salary is extremely important. However, in many cases the individual's recognition for work accomplished may be more important.

III. DEVELOPING MORALE

For good morale to exist in a group, each individual must know that they can be happy and satisfied if the other workers are happy and satisfied. This happiness is interdependent. The employee tackles an assignment with a specific level of intelligence, education, type of personality, background, and status within a group. For the morale of the individual to be high and for the group morale to be good, the employees must have their needs satisfied. They must not just belong, they must feel that they are an important part of the group and that the group would have trouble functioning properly without them. This type of morale development is difficult to control by the supervisor except for the fact that the supervisor sets the example in showing appreciation for things done. The supervisor can, however, influence the morale of the group by handling grievances in a reasonable and prompt manner and by using disciplinary action when needed in an appropriate manner. The supervisor can also influence morale by making sure the individuals receive adequate recognition for work accomplished by asking for proper wages, promotions, and other benefits for the

179

employees. An important part of developing this good morale is to have a constant flow of communication in all directions. By communications we do not mean propaganda.

As has been emphasized over and over again, the employee does not simply come to a job untroubled by his/her environment, after-hour relationships, or weekend relationships. The employee is influenced by all of these as well as by a number of other organizations and clubs to which he/she may belong. The good supervisor will learn about some of these activities without being nosey and will demonstrate a real interest and enthusiasm for the individual's concerns as well as pleasures.

IV. THE RELATIONSHIP TO PRODUCTIVITY

There is considerable evidence that suggests high morale is associated with increased employee productivity.

V. MEASURING AND IMPROVING MORALE

The level of morale can be determined in many organizations by the following techniques:

1. The amount of employee turnover.

2. The level of productivity.

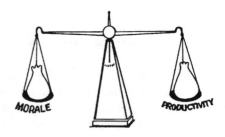

**There Is A
Delicate Balance**

3. The amount of waste and scrap material which is present.

4. The quality of records which are kept.

5. The amount of absenteeism and the days on which absenteeism occurs.

6. The amount of lateness.

7. The number and types of grievances.

8. The final comments from the employee when they leave the organization.

9. The amount and types of accidents.

10. The types of medical and emotional conditions existing.

11. The types of suggestions made by employees.

12. The level of performance in training sessions.

13. The demeanor of the individual (i.e., is the employee happy, sad, or angry).

14. The desire to innovate.

15. The quality of the work being produced.

16. The assistance that one employee gives another employee.

17. Informal interviews with the employees.

18. Opinion-attitude surveys and questionnaires which are unsigned, when filled out by the employees.

19. Unusual incidents such as industrial sabotage, theft, and so on.

In order to improve morale the following steps are suggested:

- Determine the present level of morale.

- Identify causes of poor morale.

- Determine where poor morale exists; is it in a given department or section, does it revolve around a certain supervisor, or is it simply caused by a single person or group of individuals?

- Set some plans for counteracting the poor morale. If necessary, transfer certain individuals to other jobs or provide necessary environmental conditions.

- Lower the noise level, provide better housekeeping, and so on.

- Assign an individual to the task of implementing good techniques to improve morale.

- Evaluate the results frequently and determine if shifts in technique are needed.

- Ask the employees what the best approach is to making the work situation a happier and more satisfying place to be involved in.

VI. ATTITUDES AND MORALE

Poor morale may be due to poor attitude. Therefore, by changing attitudes you may effectively apply still another technique to improve the morale of the group. An attitude is the individual's point of view. It is his/her way of looking at things. If an individual has a good attitude, it may be ruined by the supervisor constantly being on the employee's back, or by the group pressure which forces the individual to lower productivity or one's sense of accomplishment. If the worker has a good attitude but is not doing a proper job, it is important for the supervisor to be critical only in a kind way in order to help the individual as much as possible. The employee with a good attitude and poor habits might be corrected and turned into a very fine worker. An employee with a poor attitude and good habits will eventually succumb to the poor habits and become an extremely poor worker.

The supervisor is not always responsible for the employees' attitudes. After all, the employees' attitudes have been developed over many years through contacts in home life, school environment, organizations, acquaintances with people, and the pressures of everyday living. Therefore, the supervisor must recognize that all of these positive and negative attitudes have been developed over a long period of time. Negative attitudes can be changed. If they are not changed, the individual will probably need to be offered additional training, counseling, or if necessary some disciplinary action might need to be taken.

Some people are very indifferent and cannot express themselves, their enjoyment, or their needs. On the other hand, some people are extremely enthusiastic and it is important to channel their enthusiasm the proper way. It is beneficial to attempt to instill enthusiasm in the different individuals.

Despite many other things, we all are moody and at times we allow our moodiness to affect our jobs. Once again it is the supervisor's role to understand the moodiness and attempt to help individuals with problems. This will be discussed later.

Attitudes can be changed but the change will not be accomplished by preaching. New attitudes must be learned. The individual employee must recognize that poor performance receives poor reactions, and good performances receive good reactions and rewards of one type or another. Consistency should be used with the employee when he/she is attempting to change his/her attitudes. Inconsistency leads to confusion in the employee's mind and therefore prevents necessary attitude changes. Good attitudes contribute to good morale. Poor attitudes help lower morale.

VII. ELEMENTS IN MORALE BUILDING

Good morale can be built into an organization. It is reemphasized that poor morale and poor attitudes have been created in many different ways and they can be changed. During World War II the employee morale was so high that we took a peacetime economy and turned it into a wartime production line in approximately six months. If this had not occurred, we may very well have lost World War II. The steps used to build morale are as follows:

1. Determine what the employees want and what they need. Also determine

what they do not want and what they do not like.

2. Develop the employee's interest in the assignment. Fit the person to the job. Use pre-employment aptitude tests, discuss the individual's likes and dislikes, determine after a short period of time whether or not the individual seems to suit the job or if the employee belongs elsewhere.

3. Provide new tools, good equipment, and adequate supplies to carry out the job in an effective manner and to prevent frustration.

4. Develop other interests in the overall organization by providing adequate communications in all directions and by using work incentive plans and other similar methods.

5. Give the employee special incentives such as additional salary, time off, and special recognition.

6. Learn to recognize if the employee dissatisfaction is due to wages or working conditions and where it is possible, make corrections.

7. Inform the employees in a proper manner about increases or decreases in staff. Make sure that the individual realizes that he/she is not being picked on. If there is a decrease, it is due to company

policy and employee performance will be considered in layoffs. Also, the employee will be given ample opportunity for promotion, if there is an increase in higher level positions.

8. Set up legitimate after-hour activities such as bowling leagues and baseball teams.

VIII. SUMMARY

The "Fundamental Management Information" section discussed attitudes both good and bad, the supervisor's influence on behavior, behavior modification, job satisfaction, improving morale and the quality of work life.

Morale is an inner feeling the individual has. In high morale, which is really a state of independence, the individual voluntarily seeks to develop and use his/her full knowledge, power, and skill to reach a desired end. In low morale, the individual reduces or even eliminates his/her natural desire for improvement. It is difficult to measure all facets of morale and perhaps is more difficult for the supervisor to control all of these facets. However, it is the ongoing job of the supervisor to try to establish and maintain good morale which leads to happy and satisfied workers - happy and satisfied workers lead to quality and quantity products and services.

LESSON 8
CASE PROBLEM 1

The Delicate Balance

Susan Howarth, the personnel director, was informed by Emily Ames, the director, that employee productivity had dropped substantially and that there was an increasing amount of unrest among the staff of the institution. Absenteeism, lateness, and employee turnover had increased substantially. Final interviews of those leaving indicated specific problems and a general malaise in the group. If you were Susan, how would you:

1. Pinpoint specific problems.

2. Determine the present level of morale.

3. Determine where poor morale exists and why.

4. Establish a plan to improve morale.

ANSWER SHEET

LESSON 8
CASE PROBLEM 1

MANAGEMENT AND SUPERVISION FOR WORKING PROFESSIONALS

LESSON 8
CASE PROBLEM 2

The O.R. Supervisor Problem Revisited

Kim Holland had been Operating Room supervisor in the Campbell Memorial Hospital for four years. She had moved her family from their home some 200 miles away to take the position. She was highly competent and well liked. She replaced Stacy Tremain, the previous supervisor, who had also been well liked and competent. Both were BSNs from State University. Four years ago Stacy was called into Mr. Abbey's office, the hospital administrator, and was advised that she was no longer the supervisor and that she was going to become a float nurse in another part of the hospital. She was not told why this action was taken. In fact, she had been demoted without cause. She could accept the decision or leave the hospital. The O.R. nurses and techs reacted in a very poor manner to Stacy's sudden departure. There was constant griping among the staff and more and more people were out sick or late. The O.R. staff was already tense because of the surgeons, the inability to get rest during the day, or even eat lunch at a reasonable time, if at all. When Kim became the supervisor she tried to reduce the level of stress and encouraged the individuals to act as a team. She discussed each of the concerns of the staff with them and brought these concerns to the administration. The level of the performance of the staff improved. Yesterday, Kim Holland was fired as the O.R. supervisor. She was told that she would work in the education department. She could take it or leave it.

1. What effect will Kim Holland's firing have on the O.R. staff?

2. Why is the administration doing this?

3. Does the administrator owe an explanation to the individuals and staff?

4. What positive things did Kim do while she was the supervisor?

5. Did the administrator act in a fair and responsible manner in both cases?

ANSWER SHEET

**LESSON 8
CASE PROBLEM 2**

MANAGEMENT AND SUPERVISION FOR WORKING PROFESSIONALS

PRACTICAL EXERCISES

You may do any two or more of these items.

1. Determine the level of morale within your work group by setting up a worksheet utilizing the nineteen items listed in the preceding Lesson Discussion for measuring and improving morale. Determine for each individual, and the group at large, whether or not they are satisfactory, unsatisfactory, or superior in their morale in each item. Then, evaluate the checklist to see what the overall morale of the group is.

2. To improve morale, set up a checklist of the seven major items listed in the Lesson Discussion. Use each of these items in working with your group for a period of two weeks. Reevaluate the morale problem and see if it is improving.

3. Look at the attitudes of each of the workers and supervisors. Determine if their attitudes are good or bad by how they react within their working situation. Then, try to determine how best to improve their attitudes.

4. Utilizing the elements of morale building discussed in the notes, attempt to improve the morale of your working group.

LESSON 8
PRACTICAL EXERCISES ANSWER SHEET

MANAGEMENT AND SUPERVISION FOR WORKING PROFESSIONALS

Do two exercises and number them. Use additional paper if necessary.

SELF-TESTING EXAMINATION #8

TRUE-FALSE QUESTIONS (CORRECT ANSWERS APPEAR ON PAGE 191)

1. An opinion is a state of mind based on certain concepts.   1. __

2. The use of threats may be needed to get the work done.   2. __

3. In order to identify an attitude you must be able to find the behavior involved.   3. __

4. Change in itself is not a morale problem.   4. __

5. Morale is the special feeling employees have which can turn an average company into a superior company.   5. __

6. Poor morale results in absenteeism, deception, anger, hopelessness, and poor performance.   6. __

7. Rumors are an important part of the organization and are very useful in spreading information within the organization.   7. __

8. The supervisor is a major contributor to good morale.   8. __

9. The supervisor is totally responsible for the morale of the group.   9. __

10. The level of morale can be determined by the amount of employee turnover, level of productivity, and amount of waste and scrap material which is present.   10. __

11. The quality of records which are kept are based on the individual's neatness only.   11. __

12. A happy employee usually has good morale.   12. __

13. Industrial incidents such as industrial sabotage, thefts, and so on, have no bearing on the morale of the group.   13. __

14. Attitudes can be taught; therefore, a supervisor should always preach to the employees.   14. __

ANSWERS TO LESSON 8 SELF-TESTING EXAMINATION

If your answer is incorrect, go back to the material referred to and determine why your answer is incorrect.

QUESTIONS FROM FUNDAMENTAL MANAGEMENT SECTION

1. F Beginning of Fundamental Management Information
2. F Beginning of Fundamental Management Information
3. T Middle of Fundamental Management Information
4. F End of Fundamental Management Information

QUESTIONS FROM LESSON DISCUSSION

5. T Beginning of the Lesson Discussion
6. T Beginning of the Lesson Discussion
7. F Beginning of the Lesson Discussion
8. T Beginning of the Lesson Discussion
9. F Beginning of the Lesson Discussion
10. T Beginning of the Lesson Discussion
11. F Beginning of the Lesson Discussion
12. T Beginning of the Lesson Discussion
13. F Beginning of the Lesson Discussion
14. F Beginning of the Lesson Discussion

CASE PROBLEM 1 ANSWERS

The Delicate Balance

1. Conduct an employee survey, evaluate final interviews from employees, and consult with management staff regarding what they perceive may be causing the specific problems.

2. Analyze the results from an employee survey and other available data concerning absenteeism and lateness.

3. Ask employees to rate work environment, supervisors, rate of pay, benefit package, level of fairness, and job satisfaction. Leave adequate space for employees to write about specific problems. This should be a confidential survey; no names should be listed.

4. Establish a plan to improve morale by evaluating the data and then addressing the issues identified. Network with others who have similar problems. Develop a program with measurable objectives. Evaluate the plan and redirect as necessary. Always involve the staff in the program plan and analysis.

CASE PROBLEM 2 ANSWERS

The O.R. Supervisor Problem Revisited

1. It will frustrate the O.R. staff and the result will be low morale and increased absenteeism and turnover.

2. Kim Holland was probably fired because she brought the concerns of her staff to the administrator. Instead of listening to her and attempting to solve them, the administrator felt that Kim was not being supportive of the administration and simply fired her instead.

3. Yes. The individuals and staff deserve an explanation so that they can understand the objectives of the organization and their roles in it. This is an important component of job satisfaction which in turn creates teamwork and good morale.

4. She listened to input from her staff and built up the concept and reality of teamwork. She was competent herself and subsequently was a good leader.

5. NO!

LESSON 9

THE SUPERVISOR AS A COUNSELOR

LEARNING OBJECTIVES

When you have successfully completed this lesson, you should:

1. Understand that the supervisor, when acting in the role as a counselor, will not only help the individual but also help prevent grievance problems from occurring.

2. Have learned those personal traits or predictors which will alert the supervisor to potential personal problems.

3. Have learned about the personal problems of employees and how they affect their work performance.

4. Recognize some of the symptoms of mental illness and learn where to send the mentally disturbed individual for assistance.

5. Recognize both the advantages and the disadvantages of the supervisor as a counselor.

6. Recognize that counseling, on the part of the supervisor, is advice-giving.

7. Have learned when to send an individual for further assistance.

8. Recognize the concept of nondirective counseling.

9. Understand the goal of counseling.

10. Recognize danger signals in the worker.

11. Understand effective counseling situations.

FUNDAMENTAL MANAGEMENT INFORMATION

INTRODUCTION

Special employees are individuals who have personal problems which affect their related activities. These problems may include but not be limited to marital problems, chemical dependency, children, financial problems, and concerns about aging and health. They may also include work stress, poor environment, and improper supervision and management. Whereas in the lesson discussion you will learn about supervisory and management techniques used to deal with these individuals, here you will learn about the Employee Assistance Program (used by numerous employers), how it operates, and how it can effectively reduce employee problems.

EMPLOYEE ASSISTANCE PROGRAMS

What They Are - The employee assistance program (EAP) is an internal multitrack assessment and referral service for all employees and dependents. The programs are related to chemical dependency, mental health, social services, and employee work concerns. The EAP concept is that a variety of personal problems can be identified and treated successfully. The EAP office is also concerned with providing support and education to administrative and supervisory staffs in their efforts to prevent problems in the work place. An important part of an

EAP program is the promotion of a total wellness approach to daily living. The programs are operated for the benefits of both employers and employees.

How They Work - The program uses a voluntary self-referral system. The employee may request on his/her own initiative, on the advice of a supervisor, an administrator, or family member the assistance and services of the program. The individual is guaranteed that his or her position will not be jeopardized nor will an EAP referral be used by a supervisor as a means to unjustly terminate an employee. Supervisors or administrators may refer employees who are having work-related problems and those employees are expected to seek the necessary help to improve.

The EAP is administered under strict adherence to all of the provisions of ethics, privacy, and confidentiality of the medical profession. Participants are not adversely identified.

Where They Came From - The EAPs are the natural successors to alcoholism programs that were previously found in business and industry. They may be used to address the substance abuse problem in industry and government. Although initial occupational alcoholism programs were successful when dealing with individuals who were willing to be treated, they did not cover all of the needs of individuals at the place of work. The initial programs were felt by many workers to be discriminatory since the supervisors usually referred individuals to the programs. Rarely were executives, supervisors, or middle managers part of the alcoholism program although they were certainly part of the alcoholism problem.

Initially, individuals exhibiting symptoms of alcoholism were the primary users of the program. Now EAPs try to educate individuals concerning alcohol consumption, potential hazards, and techniques of intervention to be used before alcohol becomes a serious problem.

New Concerns - Drug abuse has become recognized as a problem in industry and the concern of the EAP program has had to accommodate substance abuse and chemical dependency as well as alcoholism.

Currently EAPs are concerned with identifying and assisting chronic stage substance abusers as well as individuals who may have a potential for substance abuse. These programs also assist with mental health problems and other types of psychological, medical, psychosocial, financial, interpersonal, family and legal problems.

Legal Basis for Program - The EAP programs were given a strong legal boost with the enactment of the Drug-Free Work Place Act of 1988, which requires federal contractors and grantees to certify that they will provide drug-free work places. In 1989, the Nuclear Regulatory Commission promulgated 10 C.F.R. Part 26, which is a regulation requiring any licensee authorized

to operate a nuclear power reactor, its vendors, and its contractors to institute fitness-for-duty programs. As part of this program any licensee must maintain an EAP that offers assessment, short-term counseling, referral services, and treatment monitoring to employees with problems that could adversely affect their job performance. The EAP program is designed to achieve intervention and provide for confidential assistance.

EAP policies and procedures are governed by the U.S. Constitution, Federal Law, State Constitutions and various statutes, which forbid employer discrimination against minorities, women, persons of specific ages, and handicapped people. Legal consultation is essential in developing EAP policies and procedures that are consistent with laws. Confidentiality is also absolutely essential in order to allow the individual to fully participate in the program and not to violate individual rights.

Fitness For Duty Evaluation - Where a fitness-for-duty evaluation is required by law the following signs or symptoms will be evaluated by the supervisor: (1) Drowsiness or sleepiness. (2) Odor of alcohol on the breath. (3) Bloodshot eyes. (4) Frequent trips to the bathroom. (5) Inability to concentrate or lack of attention. (6) Slurred, incoherent speech. (7) Unusually aggressive behavior. (8) Unexplained work errors. (9) Lack of manual dexterity. (10) Lack of coordination in walking. (11) Unexplained work-related accidents or injuries. (12) Unexplained changes in mood.

If the symptoms are present the individual may be removed from service and required to go to the EAP and on to further counseling or treatment programs.

Typical EAP Program - Although EAP programs vary, a typical one would include the following eight components: (1) An assessment and referral service for counseling. (2) A lunch-time learning program. (3) A health-wise newsletter. (4) A series of interpersonal skills workshops. (5) A stress lab with educational and audio-visual materials. (6) A management consultation service. (7) An operational weight loss program. (8) An adult wellness and fitness advisory committee. The goals of these programs are successful health and wellness programs for the organization. Such a program is now operating at Indiana State University. Some of the topics of the learning program include: (1) Staying healthy in an unhealthy situation, where hazards physical, mental or combination of these as well as preventive measures are discussed. (2) Aging. (3) Sexual concerns and responsibilities. A discussion of personal development and awareness. (4) Growing up male in the 21st Century. An explanation of the changing family system and changing sex roles. (5) Just how healthy are you. A discussion of our knowledge of good health practices. (6) Are you listening. A discussion of the levels at which parents, wives, or husbands listen to other members of the family and what this may do to the other individuals emotionally. (7) I am a woman. A discussion of the valuable, vibrant and current life styles of women in our society.

(8) Surviving the teen years successfully. A discussion of puberty and young adulthood containing information concerning the body and emotional and social changes and how the children as well as the parents react to this situation. (9) Coping with anger. A discussion of the emotional changes which occur when individuals grow up, are rejected, divorced, mature, or family members die.

The Health-Wise Newsletter, which is provided by the Employee Assistance Program at Indiana State University discusses human relations; drugs in the work place, legal developments; mental health; drug and alcohol addiction, disease, health hints, about the hay fever season; the stress break or job burnout; family health as it relates to chronic diseases; today's medicine as it relates to how people deal with life after 40; fitness and what value it has to you; spiritual health; consumer news, a discussion of air purifiers; laughter can be healthy; a tribute to relaxation and fun; eating for health; changing years, a discussion of how to prevent falls in the elderly, and miscellaneous section on keeping well.

EAP Director - A skilled psychiatric social worker directing an excellent Employees Assistance Program can bring considerable help to all levels of personnel within the organization, help them perform in a far better manner, and provide assistance to individuals who ordinarily would think that they are the only ones experiencing a given problem.

199

SUMMARY

Special employees can be given assistance by supervisors and managers who refer them to appropriate sources of help including the Employee Assistance Programs. An Employee Assistance Program provides confidential help and advise to employees and their families. It is also involved in many preventive efforts which should enhance family living and reduce stress and concern.

LESSON DISCUSSION

I. INTRODUCTION

The best type of supervision is carried out by individuals who motivate others to work in a willing manner. As a result of this, the supervisor works most effectively when assisting the employee instead of when demanding something from the employee. Part of this assistance is necessary personal counseling . In counseling, a supervisor tries to determine the problems of the employee, possible solutions, and the actions to be taken.

The supervisor should approach the employee by encouraging him/her to talk in order to help identify the problem. The supervisor then tries to see the problem from the viewpoint of the employee instead of from the supervisor's point of view. Finally, the supervisor should try to help develop solutions or approaches to resolve the problems.

II. PERSONAL PROBLEM PREDICTORS

The supervisor should be aware of the following ten items in order to predict the potential for personal problems:

1. Observe any unusual change in behavioral patterns such as depression, anger, sleepiness, and so on.

2. Observe the job skills of the individual and determine if the employee is suited for the presently assigned job.

3. Determine if the individual is emotionally immature. Find out why the employee is exhibiting anger.

4. Look for poor supervision which includes too little or inadequate supervision. The individual tends to lose interest as a result of this. Also, determine if your demands are too great to be satisfied.

5. Determine whether the supervisors and the employees are unable to work together. This type of friction leads to problems.

6. Determine if the individual is insecure about the job. Insecurity may be due to a variety of problems.

7. Determine if the individual is in the wrong job. If so, the person may become hostile toward all employees, to the supervisors, and to the public.

8. Determine if the individual has a series of personal problems such as domestic fights, illness, money, or alcohol.

9. Is the individual suffering from poor health or afraid of becoming sick?

10. Does the individual exhibit poor work habits? The poor work habits might be due to a lack of training or to other situations.

It is important to look at these situations and constantly have a "feel" for what is going on in the working environment. For instance, a good teacher can tell you if a student is having problems. The teacher needs only to observe slight changes in behavior which are not typical of the student.

III. PERSONAL PROBLEMS OF EMPLOYEES

The personal problems of employees may be either real or imagined. However, in either case personal problems result in reduced production and potential dissension within the occupational environment. It is obvious that everyone has problems. How we handle these problems is what is most important. These personal problems are carried into our work and unfortunately become part of the work environment. The individual who is having domestic difficulties, serious financial problems, serious illnesses, or simply has lost the ability to act as a responsible individual will cause difficulty on the job and may cause others to react in an adverse manner. We all feel a sense of inadequacy either because we have not satisfied our goals in life, have developed abnormal fears, or feel that we are not appreciated. These personal problems and the tension must be released.

A factual problem is one which really exists. The person is really unable to cope with a specific situation. There is a real lack of money or real sickness involved. A nonfactual problem is one in which the individual feels or imagines that something is wrong but, in actuality, the problem does not exist. For instance, one may feel that he/she is not being promoted because he/she is not part of the "in" group in a company. However, the real truth may be that the individual does not have the skills to warrant the promotion.

IV. SYMPTOMS OF MENTAL ILLNESS

It is important for the supervisor to distinguish between an emotional problem which might be discussed with the worker, and a potentially serious mental problem which will require professional assistance. The supervisor is not trained in handling serious problems but can be taught to watch for the following unusual symptoms in employees by asking the following.

1. Is the worker emotionally involved frequently, infrequently, or occasionally?

2. Has the worker had a sudden change in normal behavioral patterns?

3. Does the employee seem to be under considerable stress?

4. Is the employee constantly angry?

5. Is the employee constantly euphoric?

6. Is the employee tired all the time?

7. Has the employee suddenly withdrawn from the group?

8. Does the employee appear to have sharp changes in emotional behavior from sadness to happiness and back again?

9. Does the employee appear to have a considerable amount of unreasonable fears?

10. Is the employee extremely compulsive?

11. Has there been a sharp change in the employees handwriting?

12. Does the employee appear to have a sudden onset of ticks or other behavioral characteristics?

Although the supervisor does not have the specific training in psychological, emotional, or mental disorders he/she is still the first one to judge the above-mentioned changes in behavior as well as other behavioral changes. After attempting to talk to the individual, the supervisor can suggest that the worker see a physician or counselor within the occupational setting for further evaluation and assistance.

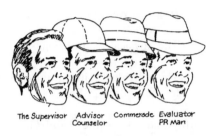

The Supervisor   Advisor   Commerade   Evaluator
                 Counselor   PR Man

The Supervisor Wears Many Hats

V. THE ROLE OF COUNSELING AND THE SUPERVISOR

The supervisor may be the first person a worker will turn to when experiencing a problem. The everyday problems of life at any given time may be overwhelming. Therefore, the worker may need to find solace from the pressure and attempt to clearly think through a solution.

These problems may include:

- Marital problems

- Alcoholism

- Children

- Financial problems

- Dissatisfaction with the job

- Problems with friends and relatives

- Concern about getting older

- Broken love affairs

- The physical environment

- The individual's inability to adjust to one's place in life

Unfortunately, one individual's problems may soon become the problem of the rest of the group. Unhappiness has a tendency to spread more rapidly through a group than enthusiasm. The role of the supervisor is to dig out these problems, attempt to alleviate the stress caused by the problems, and possibly aid the worker in resolving the problem. The supervisor can also aid the individual in getting further assistance.

VI. THE ADVANTAGES OF THE SUPERVISOR AS THE COUNSELOR

The supervisor may not have a choice as to whether he/she wants to be a counselor. However, the supervisor should know how to deal with the individual workers in a counseling situation. It is unfortunate that many people cannot handle their emotional pressures and, therefore, force them upon the supervisor. It is then the supervisor's job to make the best of the situation. Most often the supervisors have the advantage, as follows:

1. The supervisor generally knows the worker.

2. If the supervisor does not know the worker, this is an opportunity to become acquainted with the worker's manner of thinking and feeling, likes and dislikes, values, problems, and happiness. This information is of great value when the supervisor attempts to get the employee to perform at a higher level of competency.

3. From the information the supervisor receives from the employee, the supervisor learns more about the working environment he/she is supervising, the activities of various individuals within the work environment, and becomes aware of additional problems that may be occurring. The supervisor, by exhibiting concern for the individual, may motivate the employee to perform at higher levels of efficiency.

4. The sharing of a problem creates a camaraderie which may lead to better morale.

5. The investigation of the employee's problem may lead the supervisor to a better understanding of how to deal with other employees' problems and, in fact, how to deal with the supervisor's own problems. In instances where the a supervisor can act in a rapid, efficient,and effective manner, he/she can diffuse potential problems and make the working environment a happier place for all.

VII.   THE DISADVANTAGES OF THE SUPERVISOR AS A COUNSELOR

The supervisor may not operate effectively as a counselor and thereby may create more problems than are remedied. The following disadvantages should be noted:

1. The close association between the supervisor and the employee can cause problems because there are bound to be irritations, misunderstandings, and other concerns between people who work closely together.

2. The supervisor is not a trained counselor and, therefore, may overstep appropriate boundaries in counseling unless he/she knows when to make a referral.

3. In the same vein in which a doctor should not treat a member of his/her own family, it may be that a supervisor is too close to the employee to be effective as a counselor.

4. A supervisor represents authority and this may make it difficult for the employee to talk about problems. The employee may fear that the supervisor will use the employee's problem to the employee's disadvantage.

5. The supervisor may not accept the shortcomings of the employee and, therefore, cause further friction.

6. There is always danger of misinterpretation of concerns and problems.

7. The employee may reveal embarrassing or very personal information which is not the supervisors concern.

8. The supervisor may handle the situation improperly because of a lack of understanding or skill in knowing what to do.

9. The supervisor's lack of training may create other problems with the employee.

There are many advantages as well as disadvantages to the supervisor serving as a counselor. The supervisor serves in his/her role either by choice or because it is simply part of the job. A supervisor can be a very positive force in an individual's life. The supervisor can reduce the individual employee's stress, can help the employee see problems more realistically, can be someone to talk to when needed, and most importantly can help guide the employee into the proper types of additional counseling if needed.

In order to prepare the supervisor for this role, the organization should sponsor a series of seminars and one-day sessions on employee problems, proper counseling techniques, when to use them, EAPs and their role, and where and how to refer employees for further help.

VIII. COUNSELING AS ADVICE GIVING

The supervisor performs one function in counseling by giving advice to the employee. It is essential that the supervisor understand his/her own limitations since poor or inadequate advice could cause more harm than good. Because most supervisors have moved "up the ladder" to their present positions and thereby should have had more experience than the other employees, the supervisor should be able to give some advice on a number of specific problems. Once again, when the supervisor cannot give advice or when further help is required, it is essential that the employee be sent for additional assistance. Remember, any advice given should be job-related only.

The supervisor must be careful not to give incorrect, inappropriate, or harmful advice. Advice must not only be good, but it must be objective. Where the supervisor is dealing with a very specific medical, emotional, psychiatric, family, or financial problem, it is important to make the employee realize that the supervisor has been a "sounding post" and now it is time for the employee to seek more highly trained individuals for the necessary assistance.

IX. NONDIRECTIVE COUNSELING

Nondirective counseling refers to the technique in which the supervisor does not give advice to the employee but rather allows the employee to express himself/herself in order that he/she may provide his/her own solution to the problem. The employee is in a better position to know all of the pertinent points concerning the problem and in a better position to resolve it. Here, the supervisor's function is to reduce the emotional pressure and help the employee to think clearly while making decisions and arriving at solutions to problems. This type of counseling usually occurs in three stages and is most frequently practiced by the trained counselor. The three stages include:

1. Giving the individual a chance to release his/her feelings.

2. Allowing the individual to get all facts as they occurred.

3. The counselor helps the individual to assemble the facts, set forth the problems, and develop workable solutions

Since this nondirective counseling technique may be difficult to handle it is suggested that inexperienced supervisors not try to follow this technique in a strict manner.

Directive counseling, as mentioned earlier, is listening to the individual's emotional problems and helping him or her decide the best technique to use in resolving them.

X. THE GOAL OF COUNSELING

Counseling by the supervisor is a means to:

1. Produce a happier employee.
2. Reduce stress on the individual.
3. Help the person sort out his/her feelings and problems.
4. Reduce grievances.
5. Give the employee assistance in a multitude of personal areas.
6. Reduce dissension within the working environment.
7. Reduce accidents.
8. Reduce sick leave.
9. Improve production.
10. Improve morale.

XI. THE DANGER SIGNALS

Remember a supervisor must always be alert to the employee's emotional balance. The following danger signals in employees should be looked for by the supervisor in order to reduce problems:

1. Anxiety

2. Restlessness

3. Sleeplessness

4. Insecurity

5. Fear

6. Depression

7. Apathy

8. Severe self-criticism

9. Crying jags

10. Extreme excitement

11. Employee avoiding other people

12. Sudden rudeness or noisiness

13. Sudden quiet

XII. EFFECTIVE COUNSELING SITUATIONS

Before counseling can take place, the following conditions must be met. A supervisor should:

1. Assume that the employee is responsible and will continue to be responsible.

2. Understand that only the employee can change himself/herself.

3. Provide an atmosphere where the employee can express himself/herself freely. It is better to sit in front of a desk with the employee rather than having the employee in front of the desk and the supervisor behind it.

4. Express a concerned and thoughtful attitude for the employee's problems.

5. Rephrase the employee's statements so that the employee may understand what is being expressed and may define the problem more clearly.

6. Not chastise, lay blame, or criticize but give the employee quiet support.

XIII. HOW TO MAKE COUNSELING PAY OFF

The employee's performance can be improved. This has been shown in many instances where the employee has been able to express personal problems and has been able to remove them from the working environment and, therefore, has become a more efficient employee. Before the supervisor sits down to discuss problems with an employee, the supervisor must check the atmosphere of the meeting place, the time of day so that neither one will be tired or overly excited, and the privacy of the area. The supervisor should always attempt to put the employee at ease and to avoid any interruptions that may cause the employee to clam up and not express real concerns. Where necessary, a second, third, or even fourth meeting may be needed. The second, third, or fourth meeting may be important to resolve the problems or to inquire about them. The supervisor can make counseling pay off by building morale and by urging the individual to express

problems which may help others. The ultimate objective of counseling is to assist the individual in solving problems which distract from productivity and to provide a proper working environment.

XIV. SUMMARY

The "Fundamental Management Information" section discussed the employee assistance plan, how it started, what it does, legal ramifications, chemical abuse, learning programs, Health-Wise Newsletter, other problems and resources and how the program relates to management.

Although there are numerous potential drawbacks to the supervisor in the role as a counselor, the many positive aspects of this role far outweigh the negative ones. Supervision is not hitting someone over the head and forcing that person to do something. Supervision is the understanding of your fellow employees and of their problems, understanding the objectives and goals of the organization, and finally putting these all together while attempting to provide a better product or service. The effective supervisor is an effective counselor and provides necessary assistance to the employee, or provides the employee with the necessary resources to resolve personal problems.

LESSON 9
CASE PROBLEM 1

A Storm is Rising

Barry Owens, the supervisor at the Kendall Waste Water Treatment Plant in High City, had been transferred to a new division in the facility. Of the twenty people he supervised he developed a concern for Joe Banks and Dottie Hemwood, who were exhibiting some unusual characteristics. Joe appeared to be alternately depressed and angry. He did not appear to be well suited for his present job. He seemed to lose interest in his work and his level of performance fell accordingly. Dottie was unsure of herself. She was constantly worried about being laid off. From time to time strange individuals would call and ask to speak with her. She had very poor work habits and would cry if you corrected her.

1. What should Barry Owens do to determine the problem that Joe had?

2. How should he advise Joe's immediate supervisor on techniques for handling the problem?

3. What should Barry Owens do to determine the nature of Dottie's problems?

4. How should he advise Dottie's immediate supervisor on techniques of resolving her problem?

5. Are there typically other resources available that can help employees improve their performance by reducing stress?

ANSWER SHEET

LESSON 9
CASE PROBLEM 1

MANAGEMENT AND SUPERVISION FOR WORKING PROFESSIONALS

LESSON 9
CASE PROBLEM 2

A Changing Person

Bruce Sloan worked as the assistant administrator for the Select Care Nursing Home for many years. He was married and had five children, the youngest of which was thirteen years old. Tess Bane, the administrator, had noticed several unusual things about Bruce in the last several months. He ranged from euphoric to sudden bursts of anger. He seemed at times to be completely exhausted. Although always a careful worker, he now seemed to be compulsive about his work and work of the many supervisors reporting to him. He berated them when they did not satisfy him and almost immediately apologized for his actions. In the last few days, Tess noticed a remarkable change in his writing. It used to be neat and careful and now had become a scrawl.

1. What types of problems could Bruce be facing now?

2. Is his behavior affecting his work and his relationship with his subordinates?

3. What should Tess do to help Bruce?

4. Is outside help needed? If so how would you get Bruce to accept help?

ANSWER SHEET

LESSON 9
CASE PROBLEM 2

MANAGEMENT AND SUPERVISION FOR WORKING PROFESSIONALS

PRACTICAL EXERCISES

You may do any two or more of these items.

1. Utilizing the list of items under personal problem predictors, determine if there are any individuals working for you who may become a problem or who already have an existing problem. Try to determine what the problem is for the individual and then attempt to discuss it with him/her and try to achieve some results.

2. Utilizing the symptoms listed as symptoms of mental illness, determine if any of your employees who are not working properly may have some possible emotional or mental disorder. If so, refer the person to the proper counseling within the organization. Where this does not exist, discuss it with your manager to determine how best to handle the situation.

3. Recognize that people have temporary problems in life. Utilizing the list of eleven potential problems, determine if any of your employees fit into these categories. If they do, once again attempt to give them some counseling and then if necessary, move them on to further counseling or assistance.

4. Recognize both the advantages and disadvantages of the supervisor as a counselor. They are specified in the Lesson Discussion. If you find that the disadvantages outweigh the advantages, then move the individual into other types of counseling or assistance.

5. Analyze several case histories where you have given advice to employees. Make sure that your advice was good. If it was, determine if it was followed and what the results were.

6. Write down the danger signals which relate to a problem employee. Determine if the employee is giving a danger signal.

7. Read carefully the effective counseling situation and techniques and make sure that you follow these items when dealing with your next problem case.

LESSON 9
PRACTICAL EXERCISES ANSWER SHEET

MANAGEMENT AND SUPERVISION FOR WORKING PROFESSIONALS

Do two exercises and number them. Use additional paper if necessary.

SELF-TESTING EXAMINATION #9

TRUE-FALSE QUESTIONS (CORRECT ANSWERS APPEAR ON PAGE 217)

1. The EAP program is based on voluntary self-referral. 1. __

2. Employees' rights are not jeopardized by the EAP program. 2. __

3. Currently EAPs are strictly alcohol abuse programs. 3. __

4. A fitness-for-duty may be required by law. 4. __

5. A skilled psychiatric social worker typically manages the program. 5. __

6. A good supervisor gets the employees to carry out their assignments in a willing manner. 6. __

7. A supervisor should determine if the employee's problem is based on too little or too lax supervision. 7. __

8. When an individual exhibits poor work habits it is always due to his/her inability to adjust to the situation. 8. __

9. A good supervisor is like a good teacher; the supervisor can tell if one of the employees is having problems. 9. __

10. Personal problems of the employees, either factual or non-factual, have nothing to do with the working environment. 10. __

11. The supervisor is competent to determine whether or not an individual has an emotional or mental problem. Therefore, by following the items listed in the lesson discussion you should be able to make this type of determination accurately. 11. __

12. The individual's problem may spread to the rest of the group and cause a group problem. 12. __

13. Counseling by the supervisor is advice-giving and, therefore, it has its limitations. 13. __

14. Nondirective counseling refers to the technique in which the individual gives specific advice to the worker and then helps the worker resolve the problem.

14. __

15. The effective counseling situation includes the proper atmosphere and place for counseling.

15. __

16. The supervisor should lay blame and criticize when it is necessary to achieve results.

16. __

ANSWERS TO LESSON 9 SELF-TESTING EXAMINATION

If your answer is incorrect, go back to the material referred to and determine why your answer is incorrect.

QUESTIONS FROM FUNDAMENTAL MANAGEMENT INFORMATION SECTION

1. __T__ Beginning of Fundamental Management Information
2. __T__ Beginning of Fundamental Management Information
3. __F__ Middle of Fundamental Management Information
4. __T__ Middle of Fundamental Management Information
5. __T__ End of Fundamental Management Information

QUESTIONS FROM LESSON DISCUSSION

6. __T__ Beginning of the Lesson Discussion
7. __T__ Beginning of the Lesson Discussion
8. __F__ Beginning of the Lesson Discussion
9. __T__ Beginning of the Lesson Discussion
10. __F__ Beginning of the Lesson Discussion
11. __F__ Middle of the Lesson Discussion
12. __T__ Middle of the Lesson Discussion
13. __T__ Middle of the Lesson Discussion
14. __F__ End of the Lesson Discussion
15. __T__ End of the Lesson Discussion
16. __F__ End of the Lesson Discussion

CASE PROBLEM 1 ANSWERS

A Storm is Rising

1. Barry should talk to Joe and ask him if he is happy with his job and if he has any suggestions that would improve his level of performance. If there is no workable solution, it may be best if Joe is transferred to another position which is more suitable to his abilities and interests. Before such a transfer, it may be well to refer Joe to the EAP in order that he may be assisted with his problems.

2. He should ask Joe's supervisor to monitor him and document his level of performance, if it continues to decline. He should ask Joe's supervisor to try to give Joe more interesting assignments and show appreciation for work well done.

3. It appears that a lot of her problems come from her low self-esteem. She may also be having credit problems or other concerns. It would be well to also refer her to the EAP.

4. Ask her supervisor to find opportunities to praise Dottie when she does things well. The supervisor should help Dottie to plan her work and devise measurable objectives that she can meet. He should give her slow, patient, and thorough training where needed.

5. Other resources besides the EAP (if not existing at the institution) would be the personnel department, counselors, support groups, or possibly the employee medical department of the institution.

CASE PROBLEM 2 ANSWERS

A Changing Person

1. Bruce Sloan shows signs of alcoholism, drug abuse, severe emotional or mental problems, mid-life crisis, abusive behavior, loss of self-image, severe financial problems or severe family problems.

2. Yes, his behavior is having a detrimental effect on his work and people around him.

3. Tess should discuss with Bruce, in a positive manner, what is occurring, and attempt to solicit a response from him. He should be allowed to state if the allegations of others are false. If true, ask him what can be done to return him to his former productivity. It would be well to recommend that he sees a counselor or the EAP director if such a program exists at the institution. His personal problems need to be sorted out and worked on. If Bruce denies everything, but work problems continue, than professional counseling should become an important part of a plan to correct the work situation. Once the problem or problems are identified, support groups may be helpful.

Index

VOLUME I
MANAGEMENT AND SUPERVISION FOR WORKING PROFESSIONALS

MIDTERM EXAMINATION REQUEST FORM

Use this form for requesting the midterm examination. Submit form after completing lessons 1 - 5. Return the form at least **14 days** prior to your requested examination date, to insure that the examination will be in the hands of the approved supervisor on the date you desire.

Complete all information and mail this form along with a $50.00 fee to:

Independent Study
Continuing Education
Indiana State University
Terre Haute, IN 47809

Please schedule my examination on or about _____
                                                           (date requested)

Full Name	Social Security Number
Company Name	Position/Title
Address (Street, Rural Route, P.O. Box)	
City	State	Zip Code
( ) -	( ) -
Home Phone Number	Work Phone Number

Students must take their examination under the supervision of a PERSONNEL OFFICER, CHIEF ADMINISTRATIVE OFFICER, or his designate at your place of employment, a licensed SCHOOL PRINCIPAL, or superintendent, an OFFICIAL UNIVERSITY TESTING OFFICE, or for active duty military students a MILITARY EDUCATION OFFICER or Commanding Officer.

Full Name	Title/Rank
Business/School Name	
Business/School/Military Address (Street, Rural Route, P.O. Box)	
City	State	Zip Code

METHOD OF PAYMENT:	TOTAL DUE
Cash Check Credit Card Number Expiration Date	
Visa MasterCard _____ _____ _____ _____ ___/___	**$50.00**

MANAGEMENT AND SUPERVISION FOR WORKING PROFESSIONALS

FINAL EXAMINATION REQUEST FORM

Use this form for requesting the final examination. Submit form after completing lessons 6 - 9. Return the form at least **14 days** prior to your requested examination date, to insure that the examination will be in the hands of the approved supervisor on the date you desire.

Complete all information and mail this form to:

> **Independent Study**
> **Continuing Education**
> **Indiana State University**
> **Terre Haute, IN 47809**

Please schedule my examination on or about _____
                                                              (date requested)

Full Name	Social Security Number
Company Name	Position/Title
Address (Street, Rural Route, P.O. Box)	
City State	Zip Code
( ) -	( ) -
Home Phone Number	Work Phone Number

Students must take their examination under the supervision of a PERSONNEL OFFICER, CHIEF ADMINISTRATIVE OFFICER, or his designate at your place of employment, a licensed SCHOOL PRINCIPAL, or superintendent, an OFFICIAL UNIVERSITY TESTING OFFICE, or for active duty military students a MILITARY EDUCATION OFFICER or Commanding Officer.

Full Name	Title/Rank
Business/School Name	
Business/School/Military Address (Street, Rural Route, P.O. Box)	
City State	Zip Code

MANAGEMENT AND SUPERVISION FOR WORKING PROFESSIONALS

MIDTERM MAKE-UP EXAMINATION REQUEST FORM

Use this form for requesting the midterm **make-up** examination. Submit form after completing lessons 1 - 5. Return the form at least **14 days** prior to your requested examination date, to insure that the examination will be in the hands of the approved supervisor on the date you desire.

Complete all information and mail this form along with a $10.00 fee to:

> **Independent Study**
> **Continuing Education**
> **Indiana State University**
> **Terre Haute, IN 47809**

Please schedule my examination on or about _____

(date requested)

Full Name	Social Security Number
Company Name	Position/Title
Address (Street, Rural Route, P.O. Box)	
City State	Zip Code
( ) -	( ) -
Home Phone Number	Work Phone Number

Students must take their examination under the supervision of a PERSONNEL OFFICER, CHIEF ADMINISTRATIVE OFFICER, or his designate at your place of employment, a licensed SCHOOL PRINCIPAL, or superintendent, an OFFICIAL UNIVERSITY TESTING OFFICE, or for active duty military students a MILITARY EDUCATION OFFICER or Commanding Officer.

Full Name	Title/Rank
Business/School Name	
Business/School/Military Address (Street, Rural Route, P.O. Box)	
City State	Zip Code

METHOD OF PAYMENT:	TOTAL DUE
Cash Check Credit Card Number Expiration Date	
Visa MasterCard ____ ____ ____ ____ ___/___	**$10.00**

VOLUME I
MANAGEMENT AND SUPERVISION FOR WORKING PROFESSIONALS

FINAL MAKE-UP EXAMINATION REQUEST FORM

Use this form for requesting the final **make-up** examination. Submit form after completing lessons 6 - 9. Return the form at least **14 days** prior to your requested examination date, to insure that the examination will be in the hands of the approved supervisor on the date you desire.

Complete all information and mail this form along with a $10.00 fee to:

>**Independent Study**
>**Continuing Education**
>**Indiana State University**
>**Terre Haute, IN 47809**

Please schedule my examination on or about _____
(date requested)

Full Name	Social Security Number
Company Name	Position/Title
Address (Street, Rural Route, P.O. Box)	
City State	Zip Code
( ) -	( ) -
Home Phone Number	Work Phone Number

Students must take their examination under the supervision of a PERSONNEL OFFICER, CHIEF ADMINISTRATIVE OFFICER, or his designate at your place of employment, a licensed SCHOOL PRINCIPAL, or superintendent, an OFFICIAL UNIVERSITY TESTING OFFICE, or for active duty military students a MILITARY EDUCATION OFFICER or Commanding Officer.

Full Name	Title/Rank
Business/School Name	
Business/School/Military Address (Street, Rural Route, P.O. Box)	
City State	Zip Code

METHOD OF PAYMENT:	TOTAL DUE
Cash Check Credit Card Number Expiration Date	
Visa MasterCard ____ ____ ____ ____ ___/___	**$10.00**